Keynote

1

Workbook

Ben Cevik

NATIONAL GEOGRAPHIC LEARNING
CENGAGE Learning

Australia • Brazil • Mexico • Singapore • United Kingdom • United States

NATIONAL GEOGRAPHIC LEARNING | CENGAGE Learning

Keynote Workbook 1
Ben Cevik

Publisher: Andrew Robinson
Executive Editor: Sean Bermingham
Senior Development Editor: Derek Mackrell
Development Editor: Christopher Street
Director of Global Marketing: Ian Martin
Senior Product Marketing Manager: Caitlin Thomas
IP Analyst: Kyle Cooper
IP Project Manager: Carissa Poweleit
Media Researcher: Leila Hishmeh
Senior Director of Production: Michael Burggren
Senior Content Project Manager: Tan Jin Hock
Manufacturing Planner: Mary Beth Hennebury
Compositor: SPi Global
Cover/Text Design: Brenda Carmichael
Cover Photo: A bird's eye view of the High Line, New York: © Diane Cook and Len Jenshel/ National Geographic Creative

ISBN-13: 978-1-337-10414-2

National Geographic Learning
20 Channel Center Street
Boston, MA 02210
USA

Cengage Learning is a leading provider of customized learning solutions with office locations around the globe, including Singapore, the United Kingdom, Australia, Mexico, Brazil, and Japan. Locate your local office at **www.cengage.com/global**

Cengage Learning products are represented in Canada by Nelson Education, Ltd.

Visit National Geographic Learning online at **NGL.cengage.com**
Visit our corporate website at **www.cengage.com**

Printed in the United States of America
Print Number: 03 Print Year: 2022

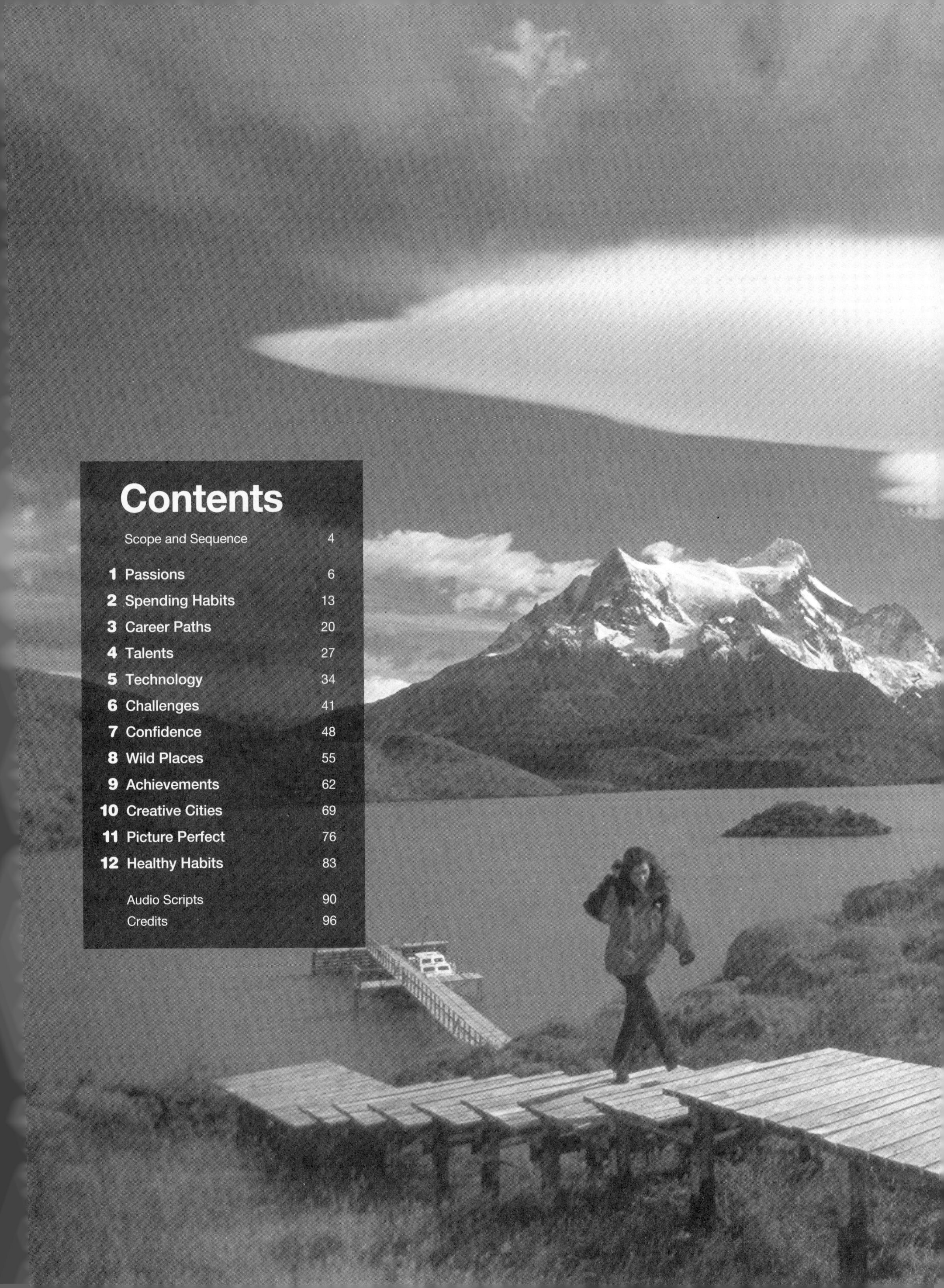

Contents

Scope and Sequence

UNIT		LESSON A	LESSON B
TITLE		**VOCABULARY** **LISTENING**	**LANGUAGE FOCUS** **LISTENING FOCUS**
1	**Passions**	Likes Talking about movies	Discussing favorites Contractions versus possessives
2	**Spending Habits**	Spending money How I spend my money	Discussing spending habits Syllable stress
3	**Career Paths**	Jobs A dream job	Discussing job preferences Intonation
4	**Talents**	Abilities A unique ability	Describing talents and abilities Distinguishing similar sounds
5	**Technology**	Gadgets My favorite gadgets	Discussing technology Homonyms
6	**Challenges**	Daily challenges It's no big deal	Overcoming difficulties Sentence stress
7	**Confidence**	Appearance and personality Describing a friend	Describing appearance and personality Contracted and uncontracted forms
8	**Wild Places**	Natural features An amazing place	Discussing natural wonders Reduced speech
9	**Achievements**	Personal achievements My great achievement	Discussing past events Past tense
10	**Creative Cities**	Qualities of a neighborhood The neighborhood where I grew up	Giving advice and making suggestions Thought groups
11	**Picture Perfect**	Photography My perfect photo	Discussing opinions /d/ sounds
12	**Healthy Habits**	Habits My healthy (and unhealthy) habits	Discussing healthy habits Linking words

LESSON C VOCABULARY BUILDING	LESSON D TED PLAYLIST	LESSON E WRITING
Collocations with *tradition*	The Art of Bow-making by Dong Woo Jang Model Rocketry by Steve Jurvetson My Journey to Yo-yo Mastery by Tomonari Ishiguro	An email
Word group: *produce*	Less Stuff, More Happiness by Graham Hill The Price of Happiness by Benjamin Wallace How to Buy Happiness by Michael Norton	Social media post
Collocations with *time*	Haunting Photos of Polar Ice by Camille Seaman Why Did I Ski to the North Pole? by Ben Sanders The Tales of Ice-bound Wonderlands by Paul Nicklen	Describing a dream job
Collocations with *talent*	A Beatboxing Lesson from A Father-daughter Duo by Ed Cage and Nicole Paris The Journey Across the High Wire by Philippe Petit Juggling as Art … and Science by Michael Moschen	Describing an unusual ability
Collocations with *engine*	I Leapt from the Stratosphere. Here's How I Did It by Alan Eustace A Leap from the Edge of Space by Steve Truglia Extreme Wingsuit Flying by Ueli Gegenschatz	A review
Collocations with *focus*	Deep Sea Diving … in a Wheelchair by Sue Austin Embrace the Shake by Phil Hansen I Got 99 Problems … Palsy is Just One by Maysoon Zayid	Facing a challenge
Collocations with *self*	Why I Live in Mortal Dread of Public Speaking by Megan Washington How I Beat Stage Fright by Joe Kowan Your Body Language Shapes Who You Are by Amy Cuddy	Describing someone
Word group: *popular*	Deep Under the Earth's Surface, Discovering Beauty and Science by Francesco Sauro My Glacier Cave Discoveries by Eddy Cartaya Life in the Deep Oceans by David Gallo	A place I'd like to visit
Collocations with *head*	Why I'm Rowing across the Pacific by Roz Savage Never, Ever Give Up by Diana Nyad My Mind-Shifting Everest Swim by Lewis Pugh	A biography
Suffix *-ate*	How I Brought a River, and My City, Back to Life by Aziza Chaouni How to Build with Clay ... and Community by Diébédo Francis Kéré Before I Die I Want to … by Candy Chang	Creative suggestions
Collocations with *dawn*	The New Telescope Might Show Us the Beginning of the Universe by Wendy Freedman Dive into an Ocean Photographer's World by Thomas Peschak A Flying Camera … on a Leash by Sergei Lupashin	Describing a photo
Word group: *globe*	Why Dieting Doesn't Usually Work by Sandra Aamodt Try Something New for 30 Days by Matt Cutts A Simple Way to Break a Bad Habit by Dr. Judson Brewer	Health tips

1 Passions

1A

VOCABULARY Likes

A Circle the correct words to complete the sentences.

1 (**Horror** / **Rock**) music usually features an electric guitar.

2 Scary movies about ghosts and monsters are called (**horror movies** / **romantic comedies**).

3 Studies show that listening to (**classical** / **action**) music helps you concentrate better.

4 (**Jazz** / **Science fiction**) movies often include robots and aliens.

5 (**Country** / **Rock**) singers often wear cowboy hats when they perform.

6 A movie about people falling in love is probably a (**horror** / **romantic**) movie.

7 A movie with violent fight scenes is probably a(n) (**action** / **romantic**) movie.

8 (**Jazz** / **Country**) music usually features a saxophone or trumpet.

B Complete the sentences using the words in **A**. Give examples for your choices.

1 I like watching ________________ movies. My favorite movie is ________________.

2 I don't like ________________ movies, such as ________________.

3 ________________ is my favorite type of music. One band/musician I like is ________________.

LISTENING Talking about movies

A ▶ **1.1** Listen to a woman describing a movie.

1 What type of movie is it?

a action **b** romantic comedy **c** horror

2 The movie is about ________.

a two chefs who fall in love and start a restaurant together

b a chef who owned many restaurants and lost his business

c a woman who overcame many challenges to become a chef

B ▶ **1.1** Listen again. Check [✓] the words the speaker uses to describe the movie.

☐ depressing ☐ sad

☐ funny ☐ entertaining

COMMUNICATION Talking about favorites

A Match each question to the best response.

1 Who's this singer?	○ ○	**a** Yes, I'm a big fan of Justin Bieber.
2 What kind of music do you like?	○ ○	**b** It's Taylor Swift.
3 Do you like Rihanna?	○ ○	**c** I hate it!
4 What do you think of pop music?	○ ○	**d** Well, I really like country.
5 Do you have a favorite singer?	○ ○	**e** Yes! I really like her!

B Answer the questions using your own words.

1 What kind of music do you like?

____.

2 What kind of music do you dislike?

____.

3 What do you think of classical music?

____.

4 What kind of movies do you like?

____.

5 Who's your favorite actor?

____.

1B

LANGUAGE FOCUS Discussing favorites

A Circle the correct word to complete each conversation.

1 Does she like action movies?	No, she (**doesn't** / **don't**).
2 Do you like rap music?	Yes, I (**does** / **do**).
3 What kind of music does she like?	She (**likes** / **like**) pop music.
4 Who's your favorite singer?	My favorite singer (**is** / **are**) Gwen Stefani.
5 What kind of movies don't you like?	I (**love** / **hate**) horror movies.

B ▶ **1.2** Listen to the questions. Choose the best response from the box.

a No, he doesn't. **b** Yeah, they do. **c** I like *The Hunger Games*. **d** Yes, I do.

1 ______ **2** ______ **3** ______ **4** ______

C Complete each conversation using a phrase from the box.

don't like it	**do you like**	**do**

1 What kind of music ____________?

Well, I like reggae, and I love dance music.

2 Do you like world music?

Yes, I ____________. It's my favorite!

3 Do they like jazz?

No, they ____________ at all. They only like hip-hop.

LISTENING FOCUS Contractions versus possessives

A ▶ **1.3** Look at the sentences below. The ones on the left do not use contractions. The ones on the right use contractions. Listen and repeat what you hear.

Not contracted	Contracted
Yes, **you are** right! I do like rap music.	Yes, **you're** right! I do like rap music.
My mom and dad **do not** like pop music.	My mom and dad **don't** like pop music.
That **is not** a romantic comedy. It is an action movie.	That **isn't** a romantic comedy. **It's** an action movie.

B Look at the example below. Contractions are different from possessives. Is each word in bold a contraction or possessive? Check [✓] the correct box.

Example: That's my brother's CD. It's Katy Perry's new album.

That's – contraction; brother's – possessive; It's – contraction; Perry's – possessive

1 Matt **Damon's** best film is *The Martian*. ☐ contraction ☐ possessive

2 His favorite **movie's** *Gone with the Wind*. ☐ contraction ☐ possessive

3 So **what's** your favorite book? ☐ contraction ☐ possessive

4 Look at my **dad's** DVDs. He has hundreds! ☐ contraction ☐ possessive

C ▶ **1.4** Listen. Circle the words that are contracted.

1 **a** are not **b** is not **c** does not

2 **a** is not **b** do not **c** does not

3 **a** we are not **b** they are **c** we are

1C

READING

Read the passage and answer the questions below.

1 Sona Jobarteh is the first female to professionally play the kora, a traditional instrument from Africa. She was born in London in 1983, but her family is from Gambia. Jobarteh has loved music since she was young. She started learning the kora when she was just three years old, and a year later she gave her first performance. Now she is one of the best kora players in the world.

2 Jobarteh's family are well-known storytellers. Storytellers play the kora while they sing, read poems, or create stories. This is an important job in West Africa, and only men used to do it. This changed when Jobarteh learned the kora. Many West Africans are now amazed to see a woman playing the instrument.

Sona Jobarteh performing at the Rainforest World Music Festival

3 Jobarteh plays concerts in different countries all over the world. She usually plays with a band that uses modern instruments like the electric guitar and drums. She sings in English and African languages while playing the kora. Her dream is to open a music school in Gambia someday.

A What is the passage mainly about?

a a band from London **b** a woman who plays an instrument **c** an African rap star

B Complete the word web using information from the passage.

Sona Jobarteh

Family: Her family comes from [1] ____________________.

City: She was born in [2] ____________________.

Instrument: She plays an instrument called the [3] ____________________. She is the first female to play this instrument [4] ____________________.

Languages: She sings in [5] ____________________ languages and English.

LISTENING

A ▶ **1.5** Listen. What is the talk about?

a African singing traditions **b** a famous musician **c** a musical instrument

B ▶ **1.5** Listen again. Circle **T** for true or **F** for false.

1	A kora has six strings, just like a guitar.	**T**	**F**
2	Part of a traditional kora is made from a type of vegetable.	**T**	**F**
3	A kora player sits down to play the instrument.	**T**	**F**
4	Kora players use one hand to pluck the strings.	**T**	**F**
5	A good kora player can make five or six sounds in one second.	**T**	**F**

C **CRITICAL THINKING** In what way is kora music similar to the bluegrass music played by Sleepy Man Banjo Boys? How is it different?

____

____

VOCABULARY BUILDING

A Complete the sentences using the words in the box.

bands	create	modern	traditional

1 ____________ instruments are often hundreds of years old.

2 Radiohead, The Beatles, and Maroon 5 are examples of ____________.

3 The electric keyboard is a ____________ instrument.

4 There are apps that you can use to ____________ music on your smartphone.

B Read the passage. Then complete the sentences using the phrases in **bold**.

England has a **rich tradition** of making folk music. For hundreds of years, parents **handed down the tradition** of singing folk songs to their children. However, in a **break with tradition**, fewer young people in England today are interested in their country's folk music.

1 For generations, kora players ____________ to their sons.

2 New Orleans has a ____________ of jazz music. Many famous players come from there.

3 Traditional country music didn't include drums. There was a ____________ in the 1930s when drums were introduced.

1D

TED PLAYLIST

THE ART OF BOW-MAKING

Dong Woo Jang is a teenager from South Korea with an unusual hobby. He enjoys building bows using different types of wood, such as maple, yew, and mulberry. Dong says that making bows is very relaxing and helps him calm down after a long day at school.

MODEL ROCKETRY

Steve Jurvetson's hobby is building model rockets. However, his rockets can actually fly up to 30 kilometers (18 miles) into the air. Jurvetson tells us why he loves building rockets and shows us some photos of his favorite ones.

MY JOURNEY TO YO-YO MASTERY

Two-time world yo-yo champion, Tomonari Ishiguro (also known as Black) was only 14 when he first picked up a yo-yo. He realized he had a natural talent for it. Black combines dance and sports to create stunning yo-yo tricks.

A What is the theme of the playlist?

a expensive passions **b** unique hobbies **c** unusual jobs

B Answer the questions.

1 Which two speakers build things? ____________________

2 How does Woo Jang's hobby help him? ____________________

3 Which speaker is a champion at his hobby? ____________________

C Circle the correct words to complete the sentences.

1 A champion is someone who (**loses** / **wins**) competitions.

2 A yo-yo is a kind of (**rocket** / **toy**). It moves up and down a piece of string.

3 A model of an object is usually a (**smaller** / **bigger**) version of the actual thing.

D Decide which talk you most want to watch. Watch it online at www.ted.com.

1E

WRITING An email

A Read the sample email to a new friend.

In the first paragraph, say where you are from and what you do.

Hi Sam,

My name's Marla. It's great to be in touch! I'm from São Paulo, Brazil. I'm 18 years old, and I'm studying music at the University of São Paulo.

In the second paragraph, write about your passion.

I'm really passionate about music, and I want to be a musician. I like all kinds of music, but my favorite is rock music. I play the bass guitar in a band called Electric Apple.

Use some new words from this unit.

In the third paragraph, ask your friend a few questions about their likes and dislikes.

How about you? What kind of music do you like? Do you play any instruments? I'd be really interested to know. Looking forward to hearing from you soon.

Best wishes,

Marla

End with *Best wishes* or *Kind regards*.

B Write an email to a new friend you met online. Answer the questions to plan your email.

1 What's your name and where are you from?

2 How old are you and what do you do?

3 What is your passion?

4 What do you want to know about your new friend?

C Now write your email. Then complete the checklist below.

- ☐ Did you use correct spelling and punctuation?
- ☐ Did you use some new words from this unit?
- ☐ Did you say what kind of music or movies you like?
- ☐ Did you ask what kind of music or movies your friend likes?

2 Spending Habits

2A

VOCABULARY Spending money

A Complete the information using the words in the box.

bus pass	coffee	haircut	shirts

I like to go shopping on Saturday. Going to town is cheap because I have a [1] ________________. In town, I usually go to a café first to have a [2] ________________. Then I start shopping. Today, I need to buy some new [3] ________________. After that, I'm going to get a [4] ________________. I'm starting a new job next week and I want to make a good impression on my first day.

B Circle the correct words to complete the sentences.

1. Let's (**have a coffee** / **get some gas**). There's a nice café just across the street.
2. It's cold today, so I'm wearing (**a jacket** / **makeup**).
3. Would you like to go to the (**concert** / **groceries**) with me?
4. I've always been interested in photography. Maybe I'll buy a (**camera** / **bus pass**).

LISTENING How I spend my money

A ▷ **2.1** Listen. What are they talking about?

a favorite shopping malls **b** money spent on clothes **c** disadvantages of shopping

B ▷ **2.1** Listen again for the keywords *spend*, *cost*, and *buy*. Complete the table.

	What they bought	How much they spent
Man	1	$50
	2	3 $
Woman	jacket	4 $
	5	$25

COMMUNICATION Talking about shops

A Circle the correct words to complete the conversations.

1 Do you ever shop at the mall?

No, I (**always** / **never**) go there. It's too busy.

2 How often do you go shopping?

Oh, I go every Saturday and Wednesday—so about (**every week** / **twice a week**).

3 Do you want to go shopping tomorrow?

(**No** / **Sure**)! Let's go in the afternoon.

4 Where do you like to shop?

I (**usually** / **never**) go to the mall near my office.

5 Why do you like shopping at Palm Mall?

Well, they (**always** / **never**) have great sales there.

B Answer the questions using your own words.

1 How often do you go shopping?

____.

2 Where do you usually go shopping?

____.

3 Do you ever go to concerts?

____.

2B

LANGUAGE FOCUS Discussing spending habits

A Cross out [**✗**] each sentence that has a mistake.

1 Do ever you shop on Main Street? ☐

2 I rarely go shopping at Pacific Mall. ☐

3 When often do you buy shoes? ☐

4 I hardly get a haircut ever. ☐

5 Do they ever buy books? ☐

B Now correct the mistakes in **A**.

C ▶ 2.2 Listen to a survey about shopping habits. Circle the best response.

1 **a** Yes, I sometimes shop online. **b** I go shopping every week.

2 **a** No, I never buy it. **b** I go to a mall about twice a month.

3 **a** Yes, I buy them every week. **b** I rarely go shopping.

4 **a** I never go shopping with them. **b** I buy some every week.

LISTENING FOCUS Syllable stress

A ▶ 2.3 In words with more than one syllable, usually one of the syllables sounds stronger. This is called stress. Listen and repeat what you hear.

For most two-syllable nouns, we stress the first syllable:

cof / fee **mu** / sic **make** / up

For most two-syllable verbs, we stress the second syllable:

be / **lieve** de / **cide** sug / **gest**

B ▶ 2.4 Complete the chart using the words in the box. Then listen and check your answers.

buy	gas	habit	mall	money
outfit	pay	shop	shopping	spending

One syllable	
Two syllables	

C ▶ 2.5 Underline the stressed syllables in the words in **bold**. Then listen and check your answers.

Example: **<u>pic</u>ture**

1 I came to **collect** my money.

2 You got a **haircut**.

3 We watched a **movie**.

4 Let's **discuss** the problem.

5 Do you like **concerts**?

6 I **begin** work at 9 a.m.

2C

READING

Read the passage and answer the questions below.

1 In 2012, British writer Samantha Weinberg was worried about the environment, and wanted to do something to help. She decided to stop shopping for one year. She only bought products she really needed, such as food, toiletries, and gas for her car. She recycled or bought everything else secondhand. This meant that she couldn't buy things like magazines, books, or toys for her kids.

2 At first, Weinberg stopped shopping because she wanted to help the environment. However, as she started looking for things to recycle, she discovered her house was full of stuff she had bought long ago but never used. She decided to donate these things to charity or swap them for more useful items. It also made her realize that she shopped out of habit, rather than necessity.

3 Weinberg faced many challenges during that year. For example, she couldn't buy birthday gifts for her family or friends. Instead of not giving gifts, she made them herself, or gave away old presents that her family never used.

4 Weinberg managed to save £5,000 at the end of that year. She also realized that not shopping resulted in more free time. She could now spend more time with the people who mattered most to her—her friends and family.

A Circle the correct words to complete the summary.

The passage is about a woman who [1](**gave up shopping / worked for a charity**) for one [2](**year / month**) because she wanted to [3](**save the environment / save money**).

B Complete the word web using information from the passage.

What she did

She still bought food, [1]__________________, and gas. She didn't buy magazines or books.

Why she did it

She wanted to help save the [2]__________________. She also had a house full of things she [3]__________________ .

Samantha Weinberg

Challenges

Weinberg couldn't buy [4]__________________, so she made them herself or gave away old ones.

Results

Weinberg saved [5]£__________________ in a year. She also had more [6]__________________ to spend with her family.

LISTENING

A ▶ **2.6** Listen. Circle the best title for the talk.

a Spending Too Much Money **b** The Importance of Shopping **c** Saving the Environment

B ▶ **2.6** Listen again. Check [✓] each statement you think the speaker agrees with.

1 People should give up shopping. ☐
2 Shopping creates job opportunities. ☐
3 The Buy Nothing New Year movement is a bad idea. ☐
4 Shopping is bad for the economy. ☐
5 Shopping has more benefits than disadvantages. ☐

C **CRITICAL THINKING** Circle the statement you most agree with. Give a reason for your answer.

a Everyone should shop less.
b We should spend more on shopping.
c Buy Nothing New Year won't make a difference.

Reason: ______________________________

VOCABULARY BUILDING

A Match each word to its definition.

1 donate	○	○	**a** something that people make and sell
2 environment	○	○	**b** a small case for keeping money and bank cards in
3 product	○	○	**c** the natural world that animals and plants live in
4 swap	○	○	**d** to give money, clothes, food, etc., to a charity
5 wallet	○	○	**e** to give something and receive something in return

B Read the passage. Then complete the sentences using the words in **bold**.

The **production** of cotton for clothes usually involves the use of chemicals called pesticides. Pesticides can make cotton farms more **productive** by killing the insects that destroy cotton plants. This makes clothes cheaper to **produce**. However, these pesticides can also make people and animals sick.

1 If you ______________ something, you make or grow it.
2 ______________ is the process of making or growing something.
3 If someone or something is ______________, they make a lot of something.

2D

TED PLAYLIST

Donating to a charity or cause might make you a happier person

LESS STUFF, MORE HAPPINESS

Graham Hill got rid of most of his stuff in an attempt to save money and become happier. He suggests three changes: First, throw away stuff you don't use. Second, buy smaller products (e.g., e-books not paper books). Third, buy things with more than one use (e.g., a table that becomes a bed).

THE PRICE OF HAPPINESS

Benjamin Wallace wanted to know if expensive things make us happy. So he tried the world's most expensive products. Did they make him happy? Not really. And nobody noticed his things anyway. He argues that expensive things—while nice to have—don't make us as happy as we think they will.

HOW TO BUY HAPPINESS

Michael Norton thinks that money can make us happy. He says that what's important is how you spend the money. Spending money on yourself doesn't make you happier—lottery winners often become less happy and get into debt. But spending money on other people or giving to charity can make you happier.

A Circle the most suitable title for the playlist.

a Does Money Equal Happiness? **b** Getting Rich the Easy Way **c** Hard Work Makes You Happy

B Complete the table.

Speaker	Main idea	Example	Advice
Graham Hill	Having fewer things makes our lives better.	He got rid of most of his [1] ________.	[2] ________ stuff you don't use, buy [3] ________ products and buy things with more than [4] ________.
Benjamin Wallace	The world's most [5] ________ products don't really make us happy.	No one noticed his expensive [6] ________.	Expensive things, while nice to have, won't always make you happy.
Michael Norton	To buy happiness, spend money on [7] ________.	People who win the lottery often become unhappy.	Spending money on yourself [8] ________ make you happier.

C Complete the sentences using the words in red.

1 ________ is another word for things.

2 A ________ is something you owe someone else.

3 To play the ________, you choose numbers and buy a ticket.

D Decide which talk you most want to watch. Watch it online at www.ted.com.

2E

WRITING Social media post

A Read the sample social media post.

Write one paragraph. Start by saying what the store is called.

Think of one or two good points about the store.

Side Two

★★★★

I think Side Two is an excellent music store. You really should visit it. I go there every weekend to look around and see what's new. They sell loads of secondhand CDs, records, and music magazines. They also sell some great comic books. I really like the staff at Side Two. They're always helpful.

Say how often you visit the store.

Remember to use words like *always*, *usually*, and *sometimes*.

B Write a social media post about a mall or store you like to visit. Answer the questions to plan your post.

1 What is the store called?

2 How often do you go there?

3 What does the store sell?

4 What do you like about the store?

C Now write your post. Then complete the checklist below.

- ☐ Did you use correct spelling and punctuation?
- ☐ Did you use some new words from this unit?
- ☐ Did you say what is good about the store?
- ☐ Did you use words like *always*, *usually*, and *sometimes*?

3 Career Paths

3A

VOCABULARY Jobs

A Match each description to a job.

1 "I teach students at a university."	○	○	**a** chef
2 "I need a camera to do my job."	○	○	**b** waiter
3 "I carry food to customers in a restaurant."	○	○	**c** pilot
4 "I perform in a theater. I need to be very fit."	○	○	**d** photographer
5 "I cook meals in a restaurant."	○	○	**e** professor
6 "I write stories about the news."	○	○	**f** scientist
7 "I fly an airplane."	○	○	**g** journalist
8 "I do experiments to find out new facts."	○	○	**h** dancer

B Complete the sentences using the words in **A**. Give reasons for your choices.

1 Which job would you like to do?

I would like to be a ________________ because ________________________________.

2 Which job would you NOT like to do?

I wouldn't like to be a ________________ because ________________________________.

3 Which job do you think is most difficult?

Being a ________________ is most difficult because ________________________________.

LISTENING A dream job

A ▶ **3.1** Listen. What is the man's job?

He is a …

a chef **b** waiter **c** manager

B ▶ **3.1** Listen again. Complete the table using information from the talk.

What does he like about his job?	What does he not like about his job?

COMMUNICATION Talking about jobs

A Circle the best response.

1 How do you like being a journalist?
a It's a fun job. I love it! **b** I write about the news.

2 Is it a tough job?
a I'd like to be a photographer. **b** It can be. I have to work hard.

3 What's your job like?
a It's really enjoyable. **b** Because the pay is good.

4 What do you do every day?
a Being a pilot is my dream job. **b** I cook food in a restaurant.

B You are interviewing someone for a school project. Complete the questions using your own words.

1 Do ______________________________?
Yes, I do. I'm a dancer.

2 Where ______________________________?
Well, I mostly work at a theater. Sometimes I practice at a dance studio.

3 What ______________________________?
Oh, I really like meeting new people and learning new dances.

3B

LANGUAGE FOCUS Discussing job preferences

A Circle the correct words.

1 Hi. What (**do** / **would**) you do?	I'm a student.
2 Do you have a job?	Yes, I (**does** / **do**).
3 Do you work in an office?	No, I (**doesn't** / **don't**). I'm a pilot.
4 What kind of job would you like to do?	(**I'd** / **I'm**) like to be a manager.
5 What don't you like about your job?	Well, I (**don't like** / **would like**) the long hours.

B ▶ **3.2** Listen to each question and circle the best response.

1 **a** I don't like my boss. **b** I wouldn't like to be a manager.
2 **a** No, I don't. **b** I'd like to be a pilot.
3 **a** I hope I get to travel a lot. **b** It's really difficult.
4 **a** I'm a dancer. **b** Oh, it's fantastic!

C Complete the conversation using the phrases in the box.

What's your dream job?	Do you have a job?
What don't you like about your job?	What do you like about your job?
What do you do every day?	

1 ______________________________

"Yes, I do. I'm a charity worker."

2 ______________________________

"I write emails and make phone calls."

3 ______________________________

"The pay isn't good."

4 ______________________________

"The hours are great, and my boss is fantastic."

5 ______________________________

"I'd like to be a pilot."

LISTENING FOCUS Intonation

A ▶ **3.3** Listen to the conversation. Notice the intonation—the way each speaker's voice rises or falls. Listen and repeat what you hear.

Do you have a job?

Do you like your job?

Yes/No questions: rising intonation

What job would you like to have?

What don't you like about your job?

Wh- questions: falling intonation

B ▶ **3.4** Draw lines to show the intonation at the end of each question. Then listen to check your answers.

1 Do you have a job?

2 Oh, great. So what do you do?

3 Mm, that's interesting. Do you like your job?

4 So, what don't you like about your job?

C ▶ **3.5** Listen to the questions and circle the best response.

1 a Yes, I do. It's great. b Well, the hours are great.

2 a I have a nice boss. b No, I don't. I'm a student.

3 a I work as a newspaper reporter. b Yes, I'm a newspaper reporter.

3C

READING

Read the passage and answer the questions below.

1 Chris Gardner was born in Milwaukee, U.S.A. in 1954. His family was poor and he had a tough childhood. When he grew up, he joined the U.S. Navy and later became a salesman. He fell in love with a woman, and in 1981 they had a son named Chris Junior (Jr). However, Gardner had to look after Chris Jr on his own.

2 One day, Gardner met a man named Bob Bridges. Bridges was rich and drove an expensive Ferrari. He told Gardner he worked in San Francisco as a stockbroker. Gardner decided then to change his career. He quit his sales job and spent time training to be a stockbroker. He worked hard but had little money. He and Chris Jr were homeless for about a year. They slept at the office, in parks, and at airports. Slowly, he saved enough money to rent an apartment.

3 In 1987, Gardner started his own stockbroking company from his apartment. The company was successful and he eventually became a millionaire. Gardner wrote a book about his life and his struggle with being homeless. The story later became a movie in 2006 starring Will Smith as Gardner and Smith's son Jaden as Chris Jr.

Will Smith and his son Jaden Smith play Chris and his son in *The Pursuit of Happyness*

A What is the passage mainly about?

a a rich man who became homeless

b a salesman who became a movie actor

c a poor man who became rich

B Order the events in Chris Gardner's life from **1** to **6**.

a ______ He had a son.

b ______ He started his own company.

c ______ He wrote a book about his life.

d ______ He and his son were homeless.

e ______ He became a salesman.

f ______ He met a stockbroker.

LISTENING

A ▶ **3.6** Listen. Which sentence best summarizes the talk?

a Finding the right job will not always make you happy.

b Too many people give up on following their dreams.

c There are some ways to make changing your job easier.

B ▶ **3.6** Listen again. Check [✓] the advice the speaker gives.

1 Ask family and friends for advice. ☐

2 Quit your current job before you look for a new one. ☐

3 Talk to people who do this job. ☐

4 Try the new job part-time first to see if you like it. ☐

C **CRITICAL THINKING** Circle the advice that the speaker and Chris Gardner would most likely agree with. Give a reason for your answer.

a It's a mistake to change your job. **b** Keep trying: never give up. **c** Believe in yourself.

Reason: ______________________________

VOCABULARY BUILDING

A Complete the sentences using the words in the box.

career	quit	routine	spend time	struggle

1 It was very difficult to get a job. In fact, it was a real ______________.

2 I ______________ studying every evening because I want to get good grades.

3 Being a doctor is usually a good ______________ with excellent pay.

4 I want to ______________ my job because the hours are terrible.

5 Her ______________ starts with a cup of coffee every morning.

B Read the passage. Then match the phrases in **bold** to their definitions.

FINDING A NEW JOB

When you have some **free time**, sit down and think about your choices carefully. Finding the right job is important, so **take your time**—don't decide too quickly. Always write a new résumé for each job application. Check it for mistakes, and send it in **on time**.

1 to take your time ○ ○ **a** happening at the correct time

2 free time ○ ○ **b** to do something carefully, not in a rush

3 on time ○ ○ **c** a time when you don't have to work

3D

TED PLAYLIST

A large iceberg near Anvers Island, Antarctica

1 HAUNTING PHOTOS OF POLAR ICE

In this talk, photographer Camille Seaman shows photos of icebergs in Antarctica. She talks about how excited she was to see an iceberg for the first time. She also explains how icebergs move and change. She says that icebergs have "lives" like animals do, changing from ice to water and back again.

2 WHY DID I SKI TO THE NORTH POLE?

Ben Saunders talks about skiing to the North Pole alone. Only three people did this before him. He completed the 1,290-kilometer trip in 10 weeks. Ben had to pull all of his food, clothes, tent, etc., while skiing. He tells some interesting stories about polar bears, bad weather, and blogging from the Arctic.

3 TALES OF ICE-BOUND WONDERLANDS

Paul Nicklen talks about photographing animals in the Arctic and Antarctic. Paul dives in very cold water for an hour to take his photos. He tells some fantastic stories about 250-year-old whales, shy bears, and a leopard seal that gave him penguins to eat. He also describes the problems that polar bears face because the ice is melting.

A What is each TED Talk about? Number the descriptions **1–3**.

a a long Arctic journey ______ **b** the nature of icebergs ______ **c** animals in cold places ______

B Answer the questions.

1 Which speaker did NOT visit the Arctic? ______________

2 How did Seaman feel when she first saw an iceberg? ______________

3 How many people did Saunders travel with? ______________

4 According to Nicklen, why are polar bears facing problems? ______________

C Circle the best answer.

1 What are icebergs?
- **a** big pieces of ice
- **b** animals from Antarctica

2 What does blogging mean?
- **a** making a phone call
- **b** writing about events and posting them online

3 If ice is melting, it is ______.
- **a** turning to water
- **b** getting harder

4 Paul's stories are fantastic. They are ______.
- **a** very good
- **b** not true

D Decide which talk you most want to watch. Watch it online at www.ted.com.

3E

WRITING Describing a dream job

A Read the sample passage about someone's dream job.

Write two paragraphs. In the first paragraph, say what the job is, where you work, and what you do.

I work as a newspaper photographer, I get to work in lots of different places, and I photograph many different things. Yesterday I was at a fashion show and today I'm taking photos at a food festival. I take hundreds of photos every day.

It's a fantastic job and I love it. I really like going to interesting places and meeting new people. Sometimes the hours are long, but I don't mind. I would like more pay, however! I think it's the best career in the world.

In the second paragraph, say what you like about the job. Try to imagine something you don't like.

Try to use some new words from this unit.

B Write a short passage about your dream job. Answer the questions to plan your passage.

1 What is your dream job?

2 What do you do every day?

3 Where do you work?

4 Why do you like your job?

C Now write your passage. Then complete the checklist below.

- ☐ Did you use correct spelling and punctuation?
- ☐ Did you use some new words from this unit?
- ☐ Did you give reasons for liking the job?
- ☐ Did you say one thing that you don't like about the job?

4 Talents

4A

VOCABULARY Abilities

A Match two words from the box to each verb below (**1–4**).

advice	decisions	directions	~~money~~
notes	soccer	tests	video games

1 make

a money ________ **b** ________

2 play

a ________ **b** ________

3 give

a ________ **b** ________

4 take

a ________ **b** ________

B Complete the sentences using the words in the box.

giving a presentation	making friends	playing tennis	taking a photo

1 I'm not good at ________________ because meeting new people makes me nervous.

2 When ________________, you need to make sure everyone is looking at the camera.

3 I love ________________—it's a great sport!

4 It's important to make eye contact with your audience while ________________.

LISTENING A unique ability

A ▶ **4.1** Listen. What can Daniel Tammet do? Circle the best answer.

Daniel Tammet can ________.

a speak hundreds of languages fluently

b remember things very well

c talk and write very quickly

B ▶ **4.1** Listen again. Circle the correct answer.

1 In (**2004** / **2014**), Tammet set a record for being able to remember a very long number.

2 He knows (**five** / **ten**) languages. He learned to speak Icelandic in (**one week** / **three months**).

3 Tammet learns things quickly by (**grouping them together** / **memorizing**).

4 Tammet is helping people improve their memories through his (**talks** / **books**).

COMMUNICATION Talking about abilities

A Read the conversation. Replace the words in **bold** with words from the box.

not bad	that good	terrible	very nice

A: Hi! I heard you singing. You're amazing!

B: Thanks, that's **really kind** of you. Do you sing? 1 ______

A: Yeah, but I'm not **very good** at it. I play the guitar though. 2 ______

B: Well, that's great! I'm **really bad** at guitar. 3 ______

A: Maybe I can play while you sing. I'm **pretty good** at folk music. 4 ______

B Complete the sentences using your own words.

1 What sport are you good at?

______.

2 Are you good at giving presentations?

______.

3 What is one thing you are not very good at?

______.

4B

LANGUAGE FOCUS Describing talents and abilities

A Match each question to the best response.

1 Are you good at sports? ○	○ a No, I don't.
2 Do you know how to ride a bicycle? ○	○ b Yes, I can.
3 Can you cook? ○	○ c I can play the piano.
4 What instrument can you play? ○	○ d Yes, I am.

B Unscramble the words to make questions. Then answer the questions using your own words.

1 drive a car / know how to / Do you ______?

______

2 photos / good at / Are you / taking ______?

______

3 underwater / you / Can / swim ______?

______

C 4.2 Listen to the conversation. Answer the questions.

1 Can the man speak Spanish?

____

2 Is the woman taking Spanish lessons?

____

3 Is the man going to South America?

____

4 Can the woman play the guitar well?

____

LISTENING FOCUS Distinguishing similar sounds

A 4.3 Some words sound the same except for one sound. We call these *minimal pairs*. Listen and repeat what you hear.

sit	seat
see	she
disk	desk

B 4.4 Match the minimal pairs. Look up the meanings of words you don't know. Then listen and check your answers.

1 ship ○	○ **a** pen
2 bat ○	○ **b** set
3 sat ○	○ **c** sheep
4 pan ○	○ **d** bet
5 fit ○	○ **e** feat
6 bin ○	○ **f** been

C 4.5 Listen to each sentence. Which word does the person say? Circle the correct answer.

1 a sat	**b** set
2 a pen	**b** pan
3 a send	**b** sand
4 a slip	**b** sleep
5 a bat	**b** bet
6 a ship	**b** sheep

4C

READING

Read the passage and answer the questions below.

1 Want to make money using social media? Then turn your talent into income by posting your work online. Here are two people who tried it and succeeded.

The Painter

2 Katie Rodgers always loved painting beautiful clothes and decided to share a few photos of her work online. Big fashion brands noticed her paintings and wanted her to create more designs featuring their clothes. She quit her office job when she started earning much more through her online business. The key to her success? "It's not enough to have talent," she says. "You need passion."

The Dog Lover

3 Shirley Braha takes photos of her dog, Marnie, and posts them on Instagram. Over a million people follow her online. She makes money from calendars and videos featuring Marnie. In fact, she makes as much money as she used to while working full-time—but she says her new job is more fun. "There's stress that comes with it," she says, "but it's fun stress."

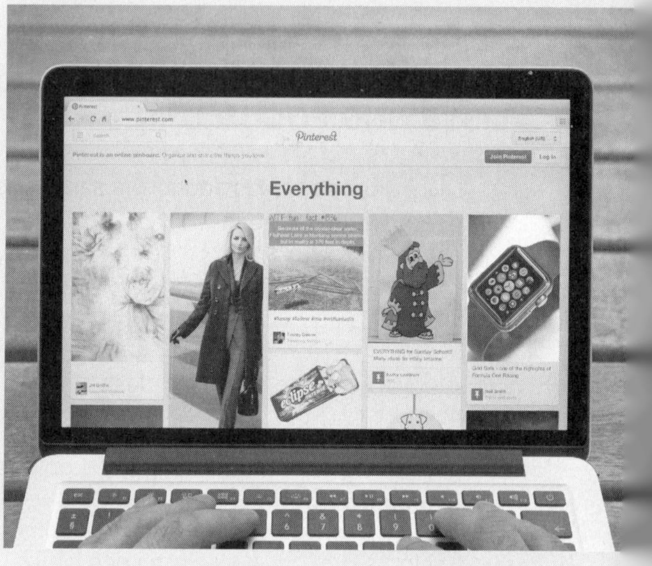

Social media isn't just for staying connected with friends, but can also be a means to earn an income.

A What is the passage mainly about?

a using the Internet to earn money from your hobby

b the importance of teaching your skills to other people

c how to have fun while earning money

B Circle the correct answer.

1 Why did Rodgers quit her job?

- **a** Her online business was more successful.
- **b** She was having too much fun with her online business.
- **c** Big brands wanted to hire her.

2 Which statement is true?

- **a** Braha makes more money now, but her old job was more fun.
- **b** Braha's hobby can be stressful at times, but she enjoys it a lot.
- **c** Braha mostly posts photos of her dog that were taken by other people.

LISTENING

A ▶ **4.6** Listen. What is the speaker talking about?

a finding classes online **b** learning about new hobbies **c** earning money from a hobby

B ▶ **4.6** Listen again. Answer the questions.

1 Number (**1–3**) the advice given in the talk.

a Teach people how to do your hobby. ________

b Make a product and sell it. ________

c Share what you do on the Internet. ________

2 Which example does not match the advice given in the talk?

a "I have a travel blog. Sometimes hotels advertise their promotions on my page."

b "I love gardening. I sell fresh vegetables from my garden at the farmers' market."

c "I love playing the piano. I often look for new songs to learn on the Internet.

C **CRITICAL THINKING** Check [✓] each piece of advice from the talk that Rodgers and Braha followed.

☐ Turn your hobby into a job.

☐ Teach people how to do your hobby.

☐ Share your talent on the Internet.

☐ Make a product using your hobby.

VOCABULARY BUILDING

A Complete the information using the words from the box.

advertisements	**injury**	**retire**	**stress**	**tournaments**

In 1997, Tiger Woods became the world's number one golfer. Nine years later, at age 30, he won the Buick Open and became the youngest player to win 50 [1]________. However, in 2010, he lost several games because of [2]________ caused by family problems. He then suffered from a back [3]________ in 2014 and had to stop playing for some time. Woods is still one of the world's best-paid sportspeople. In 2015, he made about $50 million, mostly from playing in competitions and making [4]________. He says he will continue to play and has no plans yet to [5]________.

B Read the passage. Then complete the sentences below using the phrases in **bold**.

You've probably seen a **talent show**, such as *America's Got Talent*. In these shows, ordinary people appear on TV to reveal their **hidden talents** to the world. A few have their **raw talent** recognized and become stars, but most go home in tears.

1 A ________ is a talent that no one knows you have.

2 People with ________ didn't learn their talent—they have it naturally.

3 In a ________, people try to show how well they can perform.

TEDTALKS

4D

TED PLAYLIST

Philippe Petit walking across a tightrope between the World Trade Center's Twin Towers in 1974

A BEATBOXING LESSON FROM A FATHER-DAUGHTER DUO

Ed Cage and Nicole Paris are a father and daughter beatboxing team. When Nicole was a baby, Ed beatboxed to help her sleep. Now they compete to find out who sounds better. And they beatbox just about everywhere—in the kitchen, in the car, and even in church!

THE JOURNEY ACROSS THE HIGH WIRE

Philippe Petit (pictured above) started tightrope walking at the age of 16 after seeing it performed at a circus. Petit talks about his greatest achievement—tightrope walking between the Twin Towers of the World Trade Center, 400 meters up in the air!

JUGGLING AS ART ... AND SCIENCE

Michael Moschen tells us that juggling can be fun. But, he says, it's more than just throwing and catching balls. He shows us how juggling can teach us about art and science—using skill, space, and rhythm.

A Circle the best title for the playlist.

a People Who Have Dangerous Hobbies

b Talents You Can Learn In A Day

c People With Entertaining Talents

B Match the quotes to the speakers.

1 Ed Cage and Nicole Paris ○

2 Philippe Petit ○

3 Michael Moschen ○

○ **a** "I approach the edge. I step over the beam. I put my left foot on the cable…"

○ **b** "Part of the challenge was to try to understand rhythm and space using not just my hands… but using the rhythm of my body and feet, and controlling the balls with my feet."

○ **c** "Then you would see a rapper, and when the rapper began to rap, we would do a simple beat…"

C Complete the sentences using the words in red.

1 A(n) ____________ is something that someone has succeeded in doing after a lot of effort.

2 A(n) ____________ is a group of people who work together.

3 If you ____________ something, you learn something you did not know before.

D Decide which talk you most want to watch. Watch it online at www.ted.com.

4E

WRITING Describing an unusual ability

A Read the sample paragraph about one person's special talent.

Write one paragraph. Start by saying who the person is and what their talent is.

Remember to use *can* and new words from this unit.

My friend Juanita has a fantastic talent. She can speak six languages, and she can learn a new language in a month. She works as a translator, turning one language into another. She often helps tourists who are in trouble and gives language lessons to children for free.

Say how the person makes money out of their talent.

Say how the person helps others using this talent.

B Write a paragraph about someone you know who has an unusual ability or talent. Answer the questions to plan your paragraph.

1 Who is the person?

2 What is their ability or talent?

3 How does the person make money from their talent?

4 How does the person help other people with this talent?

C Now write your paragraph. Then complete the checklist below.

- ☐ Did you use correct spelling and punctuation?
- ☐ Did you use some new words from this unit?
- ☐ Did you describe what the person does?
- ☐ Did you describe how the person helps others using their talent?

5 Technology

5A

VOCABULARY Gadgets

A Circle the correct words to complete the descriptions.

Personal drone

Personal drones are really [1](**expensive** / **fun**) because you can enjoy them anywhere. Some drones are very [2](**strong** / **light**)—weighing only 100 grams. Despite their small size, these drones can fly very [3](**fast** / **high**), with a top speed of 50 kilometers per hour!

Smartwatch

A smartwatch is a(n) [4](**modern** / **old**) version of the traditional watch. They are usually [5](**expensive** / **thin**), costing hundreds of dollars. You can do many things with a smartwatch, like play music or answer calls. A smartwatch is really [6](**light** / **easy to use**)—you just speak a command, and it does what you want.

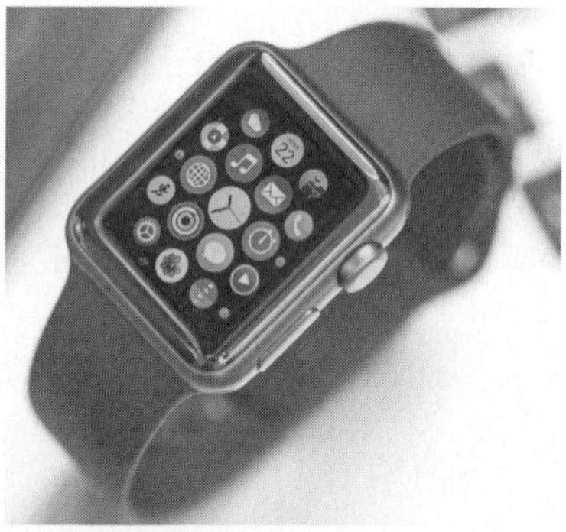

Tablet

Tablets these days are really [7](**fast** / **thin**)—with some measuring only 5 millimeters from front to back. They're also very [8](**easy to use** / **strong**). So even if you sit on one, it won't break!

B Answer the questions using your own words.

1 What is your favorite gadget? Why?

____

2 What gadget do you really want? Why?

____

3 Which are better, tablets or smartphones? Why?

____

LISTENING My favorite gadgets

A 5.1 Listen. Circle the best answer.

1 What is the gadget being reviewed?

a a smartwatch **b** a smart TV **c** a smartphone

2 What was the rating given by the reviewer?

a three stars **b** four stars **c** five stars

B 5.1 Listen again. Complete the chart below using information from the talk.

Good points	It can be connected to the [1] ______________. The display is very [2] ______________. It's very [3] ______________, measuring only 3 centimeters in thickness.
Bad points	It's very [4] ______________ compared to other smart TVs. The menus are confusing. It is very [5] ______________ and difficult to move around.

COMMUNICATION Talking about gadgets

A Complete the conversation. Number the sentences (**1–6**) in the correct order.

a ______ Yeah, I just bought it last week.

b ______ Not really. I only paid $300 for it.

c ______ Wow! That's quite useful. Was it very expensive?

d __1__ Hey, is that a new smartphone?

e ______ It looks really nice. Can it do any cool stuff?

f ______ Well, it has an underwater camera. And, there's a built-in fitness app.

B Think about a gadget you own. Answer the questions using your own words.

1 What is the gadget?

____

2 What do you think of it?

____

____

3 What does it do?

____

____

5B

LANGUAGE FOCUS Discussing technology

A Circle the correct option to complete each sentence.

1 My smartphone ______ photos.

a can take **b** to take

2 That e-reader only has a ______ books on it.

a few **b** little

3 He uses his tablet ______ emails.

a sending **b** to send

B Complete the conversation using *many* or *much*.

A: Your new phone plays music, doesn't it? How [1]______________ songs can you put on it?

B: Oh, hundreds. But I don't have [2]______________ music to put on it.

A: Well, do you have [3]______________ games?

B: Two or three, I think. To be honest, I don't have [4]______________ time to play games.

C 5.2 Listen to each question and circle the best response.

1 **a** It can record TV shows. **b** It's very expensive.

2 **a** It can't record videos. **b** I use it to watch movies online.

3 **a** It cost $1,000. **b** It doesn't have much memory.

LISTENING FOCUS Homonyms

A 5.3 Some words sound the same, but have different meanings. Usually the spellings are different. We call these *homonyms*. Listen and repeat what you hear.

I **know** there are **no** game consoles in the shop.
I've been feeling very **weak**. I was sick for almost a **week**.
Is there a phone around **here**? I can **hear** it ringing.

B 5.4 Match the homonyms. Listen and check your answers.

1 I ○	○ **a** mail
2 hi ○	○ **b** eye
3 knew ○	○ **c** high
4 male ○	○ **d** new

C 5.5 Listen to each sentence. Which word does the person say? Circle the correct answer.

1 **a** ate **b** eight

2 **a** cent **b** sent

3 **a** knows **b** nose

4 **a** son **b** sun

5C

READING

Read the passage and answer the questions below.

1 Many of us fly regularly, but how many of us can do it using just our bodies? A Canadian team has done just that with a human-powered helicopter called the Atlas. The huge helicopter won't take you very far though—it can only lift three meters off the ground, and it can't fly outdoors.

2 Three meters might not sound very impressive, but it is an achievement—since human-powered helicopters were thought to be impossible to build. People have dreamed about human-powered flight for thousands of years. And to date, only five successful human-powered helicopters have been built.

3 The Atlas needs very big wings, or blades, to keep it in the air and to stop it from falling to the sides. It has eight blades, each one measuring five meters long. The blades turn slowly, and making them turn isn't easy. The pilot sits on a bicycle and pedals hard. To steer, he leans from side to side.

4 "This isn't something that you're going to commute to work in any time soon," says the pilot Todd Reichert, "but it's about pushing the limits … and what you can do with really creative design."

A Choose the best title for the passage.

a Building Cheap Helicopters **b** The World's Fastest Helicopter **c** A Helicopter without an Engine

B Complete the information using words from the passage.

The helicopter is called [1] ____________. It can hover [2] ____________ meters in the air. It has eight [3] ____________. Each one measures [4] ____________ meters. Todd Reichert is the [5] ____________. He sits on a [6] ____________ and [7] ____________ very hard to make the blades turn.

LISTENING

A ▶ **5.6** Listen. What is the talk mainly about?

a a flying competition **b** a powerful helicopter **c** a helicopter pilot who won a competition

B ▶ **5.6** Listen again. Circle **T** for true and **F** for false.

1 The competition started in 2013. **T** **F**

2 The initial prize money was $25,000. **T** **F**

3 For 15 years, nobody participated in the competition. **T** **F**

4 The Atlas team won $25,000. **T** **F**

C **CRITICAL THINKING** Since the Atlas team's win, do you think more inventors will participate in the competition? Give one reason to support your answer.

____

VOCABULARY BUILDING

A Complete the information using the words in the box.

engine	equipment	fuel	parachute	steer

The Aerochute is a small aircraft. Instead of wings, it has a(n) [1]__________ above it. This makes it very safe. If the [2]__________ stops, the Aerochute slowly falls to the ground. It carries 29 liters of [3]__________—enough to fly for two hours. It is easy to control: You [4]__________ the Aerochute by pulling handles on the left and right. The aircraft can carry up to 100 kilograms of [5]__________.

B Read the passage. Then complete the sentences using the words in **bold**.

If you type "airplane accident" into a **search engine**, you will find many stories about planes having **engine trouble** or crashing. However, thanks to modern **engineering**, planes are now equipped with the latest safety features—making flying much safer than before.

1 __________ students learn about how machines work.

2 *Google* is an example of a popular __________.

3 A person usually sends his or her car to a mechanic if it has __________.

An Aerochute is very easy to navigate and is built to safely carry its passengers.

5D

TED PLAYLIST

Ueli Gegenschatz BASE jumping from a rock tower in Switzerland

I LEAPT FROM THE STRATOSPHERE. HERE'S HOW I DID IT

In 2014, Alan Eustace jumped from the stratosphere—40 kilometers above the Earth's surface. It was the highest parachute jump ever attempted. Alan used a special suit to protect him from the cold. Alan talks about what he experienced dropping back to Earth at 1,300 kilometers per hour.

A LEAP FROM THE EDGE OF SPACE

Steve Truglia talks about the stunts he does for movies. They include car crashes and being on fire. Steve now plans to do a parachute jump from the stratosphere. With little oxygen and temperatures below -50°C, he will need a suit similar to an astronaut's.

EXTREME WINGSUIT FLYING

Ueli Gegenschatz (pictured above) does extreme sports in a wingsuit. He jumps off mountains, bridges, and buildings and can reach speeds of 160 kilometers per hour before landing with a parachute. Ueli talks about why he loves flying and how he controls a wingsuit. He says he wants to set a new record for the longest distance flown in a wingsuit.

A Circle the best theme for the playlist.

a high-tech fliers **b** amazing movie technology **c** going into space

B Use the information (**a**–**e**) to complete the Venn diagram.

a broke a record or wants to break a record

b wears a special suit

c jumped or plans to jump from the stratosphere

d jumps off mountains

e performs stunts in movies

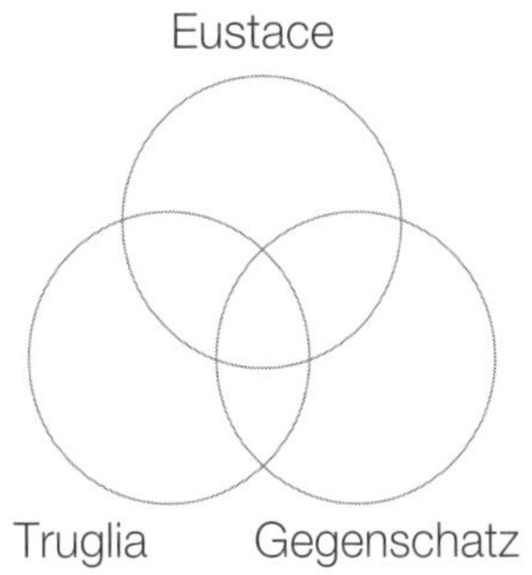

C Complete each sentence using the correct form of the words in red.

1 I saw a(n) __________ in a movie where a man jumped out of a burning helicopter.

2 There's no __________ in space, so we can't breathe there.

3 Yves Rossy wears a helmet to __________ his head.

D Decide which talk you most want to watch. Watch it online at www.ted.com.

5E

WRITING A review

A Read the sample review about a gadget.

Write two paragraphs. In the first paragraph, say what the product is and what it does.

Use some new words from this unit.

★★★★☆ — Give the app, gadget, or video game a rating out of five.

I recently bought a new smartphone. As well as making calls and sending messages, it can take really clear photos and make some great videos. I also use it to play music.

It's very attractive, light, and quite cheap. It has a lot of apps. The best is a fitness app that lets me track my activity level each day. The only problem is that it's slow. It also doesn't have much memory, so I can't store too many photos or videos on it.

In the second paragraph, describe its good and bad points.

B Write a review about an app you have used. Answer the questions to plan your review.

1 What app is it?

2 What can it do?

3 What are the app's good points?

4 What are the app's bad points?

C Now write your review. Then complete the checklist below.

☐ Did you use correct spelling and punctuation?

☐ Did you describe the app's good and bad points?

☐ Did you describe the app?

☐ Did you give the app a rating?

6 Challenges

6A

VOCABULARY Daily challenges

A Complete the sentences using the words in the box.

friends	health	money	pressure	stress

1 When you want to buy something, you pay with ________________.

2 It was very difficult to leave my ________________ behind when I moved to the city.

3 Too much ________________ from your teachers to study hard could cause you to suffer from ________________.

4 You should go to the doctor regularly to make sure you are in good ________________.

B Answer the questions using the words from **A**.

1 What is one of your biggest challenges this year?

One challenge is ____.

2 What is usually not a problem for you?

________________________________ is usually not a problem for me.

3 Who puts pressure on you? What do they pressure you about?

________________ pressures me about ________________________________.

LISTENING It's no big deal

A ▶ 6.1 Listen to the talk and answer the questions.

1 What is the talk mainly about?

a saving money

b work stress

c the toughest job

2 Which of these is considered a stressful job?

a pilot

b professor

c librarian

B ▶ **6.1** Listen again. Complete the table below using information from the talk.

What causes work stress?	Stress causes health problems such as ...	What can you do?
• working [1]__________ without a break • worrying about [2]__________ your job	• tiredness • depression • weight [3]__________	• take [4]__________ breaks • take up a [5]__________

COMMUNICATION Talking about challenges

A Complete the conversation. Number the sentences (**1–5**) in the correct order.

a ______ Sounds like you've been having a tough time. How do you manage?

b __1__ Hi! How are you? I haven't seen you in quite a while.

c ______ That's good. But you should also try to find some time to relax!

d ______ Oh, hi! I've been busy trying to cope with my work and studies.

e ______ Well, I recently cut down my work hours. And I joined a study group to get some help with my lessons.

B Answer the questions using your own words.

1 What is challenging about learning English?

__________________________________ is challenging for me.

2 How do you deal with this challenge?

One thing I do is ____.

6B

LANGUAGE FOCUS Overcoming difficulties

A Read the sentences below. Cross out [**✗**] each sentence that has a mistake.

1 Have your breakfast before you go to school. ☐

2 Listen to then some relaxing music. ☐

3 Take a deep breath you when feel stressed. ☐

4 Do something after relaxing your exam. ☐

B Now correct the mistakes in **A**.

C ▶ 6.2 Listen. Circle the correct words to complete the sentences.

1 The speaker takes deep breaths (**after** / **before**) he arrives at work.

2 The speaker listens to relaxing music (**after** / **before**) having a meeting.

3 The speaker tells his manager (**when** / **before**) he has too much work.

4 The speaker finishes work (**before** / **when**) she goes to the gym.

LISTENING FOCUS Sentence stress

A ▶ 6.3 *Stress* can tell us what the speaker thinks is important. Listen and repeat what you hear.

- **Carl** doesn't worry after exams. (Another person worries, not Carl.)
- Carl doesn't worry **after** exams. (Carl probably worries *before* exams.)

B ▶ 6.4 Circle the word that should be stressed in each response. Then listen and check your answers.

1 **Q:** Did you fail your English exam?
A: No, I failed my math exam.

2 **Q:** Does Andrew study English on Mondays?
A: No, he studies Spanish on Mondays.

3 **Q:** Did you help Sam study for his driving test?
A: No, I helped Rachel study for her driving test.

4 **Q:** Are they going to the movie on Saturday?
A: No, they're going on Sunday.

5 **Q:** Was Simon involved in the accident?
A: No, his sister was in the accident.

C ▶ 6.5 Listen to the stress in each question. Choose the best response.

1 Are you meeting David at the coffee shop?
a No, I'm meeting him at the restaurant.
b No, I'm meeting James there.

2 Does Lee play the guitar?
a No, he plays the piano.
b No, Sam plays the guitar.

3 Did Julie go to the supermarket?
a No, she went to the library.
b Yes, she did.

4 Was his mother at the game?
a No, his father was.
b Yes, she was.

6C

READING

Read the passage and answer the questions below.

1 On October 31, 2003, tragedy struck surfer Bethany Hamilton. While surfing at Tunnels Beach, Hawaii, a shark bit off her left arm. With the help of a friend, the 13-year-old bravely paddled back to shore with her good arm and was rushed to the hospital. While recovering, she was determined to get back into the water again. Amazingly, she surfed again—just 26 days after her shark attack.

2 Hamilton's recovery was painful. She had to learn to surf with one arm. She developed a new technique—kicking more with her legs—and used a surfboard with a handle so that she could hold on. Just two years after the shark attack, Hamilton won the NSSA National Championship. Since then, she's also won many other competitions.

3 In 2004, Hamilton wrote a book about her life. Inspired by her courage, *Soul Surfer*, a movie about Hamilton, was made in 2011. Her advice for people who face challenges: "Set your mind to whatever you want to do and put a good attitude in it … you can succeed."

Bethany Hamilton surfing at the Roxy Pro women's surf competition in 2005

A What is the passage about?

a a movie that was inspired by a shark-attack victim

b a shark that attacked a surfer in Tunnels Beach, Hawaii

c a shark-attack victim who became a championship surfer

B Match each event to the correct year. One year is extra.

1 Hamilton won a major surfing championship.	○	○ **a** 1990
2 Hamilton wrote about her life experiences in a book.	○	○ **b** 1992
3 A shark attacked her and bit off her arm.	○	○ **c** 2003
4 *Soul Surfer*, a movie about Hamilton's life, was released.	○	○ **d** 2004
5 Hamilton was born.	○	○ **e** 2005
		○ **f** 2011

LISTENING

A ▶ **6.6** Listen. What is the talk mainly about?

a a doctor who treats people with climbing injuries

b how a rock climber learned to climb again

B ▶ **6.6** Listen again. Circle the correct answer.

1 What happened to Herr?

a He was born without legs. **b** He lost his legs in an accident.

2 How did Herr overcome his disability?

a He designed special legs to help him climb. **b** He learned to climb using just his hands.

3 How is Herr helping others?

a He teaches rock-climbing classes for people with disabilities. **b** He designs robotic legs for people with disabilities.

C **CRITICAL THINKING** Who would most likely say each statement? Write **B** for Bethany, **H** for Hugh, or **BH** for both.

1 "I didn't give up after something bad happened." ______

2 "Many people were inspired by my book." ______

3 "My job involves helping other people with disabilities." ______

VOCABULARY BUILDING

A Circle the correct answer.

1 Your **brain** is the part of your body that ______.

a controls your thoughts **b** that you use to eat

2 To **focus on** something means to ______.

a forget about it **b** pay attention to it

3 If something is **reflected**, it hits a surface and ______.

a bounces back **b** breaks

4 Your **surroundings** are everything ______ you.

a around **b** behind

5 If you **remove** something, you ______.

a take it away **b** put it back

B Read the definitions below. Then complete the sentences using the words in **bold**.

main focus: the person or thing that gets the most attention

comes into focus: to notice something and start paying attention to it

out of focus: something that cannot be seen clearly

1 All the pictures were not clear because the camera was ______________.

2 The issue of poor health care usually ______________ during elections.

3 The ______________ of last week's meeting was work-related stress.

6D

TED PLAYLIST

Sue Austin performs acrobatic underwater acts in her special wheelchair

DEEP SEA DIVING ... IN A WHEELCHAIR

After an illness left her unable to walk, Sue Austin had to learn how to use a wheelchair. For Austin, getting a wheelchair meant freedom. It was like "an enormous new toy." She decided to change people's opinions of wheelchairs—by making one that works underwater!

EMBRACE THE SHAKE

Phil Hansen was studying art when his hands started shaking. He could no longer draw so he quit art school. One day, he drawing again—despite his shaking hands. He found his drawings were different than before but in a good way. He talks about how he accepted his limitation and used it to change his life.

I GOT 99 PROBLEMS ... PALSY IS JUST ONE

Maysoon Zayid has cerebral palsy, which makes it difficult for her to control her movements. Doctors told her she would never walk, but after many years of fighting her disability, she is now able to walk. She describes her life in this funny talk.

A What is the theme of the playlist?

a overcoming physical disabilities **b** comedians who face challenges **c** living with cerebral palsy

B Circle the correct answer.

1 "I could move around and feel the wind in my face again. Just being out on the street was exciting." Which speaker most likely said this?

a Sue Austin **b** Phil Hansen

2 Phil Hansen had to _______ .

a change his career because of his disability. **b** learn to draw differently because of his disability.

3 "I learned how to dance in heels, which means I can walk in heels." Which speaker most likely said this?

a Sue Austin **b** Maysoon Zayid

C Complete each sentence using the words in red.

1 Something that is _____________ is very big or large.

2 People who can't walk sometimes use a(n) _____________ to help them move around.

3 Being deaf wasn't a(n) _____________ for Beethoven. He still wrote excellent music.

D Decide which talk you most want to watch. Watch it online at www.ted.com.

6E

WRITING Facing a challenge

A Read the sample passage about someone who overcame a challenge.

Write two paragraphs. In the first paragraph, describe the challenge faced and its effects.

My sister had a problem saving money. At the end of every month, her bank account was always empty. It made her feel very stressed. She spent too much money on online shopping. She decided to do something to stop this habit.

Use some new words from this unit.

In the second paragraph, describe how the person overcame the challenge.

She came up with a budget and stopped spending so much money on shopping. She also got a part-time job and started saving money every month. After two years, she had saved enough to buy a car.

Remember to use *before, after, then*, etc.

B Write about a challenge you overcame in your life. Answer the questions to plan your passage.

1 What is the challenge?

2 What effect did the challenge have on you?

3 How did you plan to overcome the challenge?

4 What was different after you overcame the challenge?

C Now write your passage. Then complete the checklist below.

- ☐ Did you use correct spelling and punctuation?
- ☐ Did you use sequencing words like *after* and *before* correctly?
- ☐ Did you use some new words from this unit?
- ☐ Did you describe the challenge and how you overcame it?

7 Confidence

7A

VOCABULARY Appearance and personality

A Match each statement to an adjective that describes the person.

1 "She's very beautiful."	○	○	**a** easygoing
2 "My brother never shares his stuff."	○	○	**b** funny
3 "My friend gets nervous about meeting new people."	○	○	**c** handsome
4 "He is always relaxed and never gets upset."	○	○	**d** pretty
5 "My sister talks all the time."	○	○	**e** selfish
6 "She makes people laugh all the time."	○	○	**f** short
7 "Everyone in my class is taller than I am."	○	○	**g** shy
8 "He's very good-looking."	○	○	**h** talkative

B Answer the questions using your own words.

1 Describe your appearance.

____

____

2 Describe your best friend's personality.

____

____

LISTENING Describing a friend

A ▶ **7.1** Listen. Who is Angela describing?

a her friend

b her sister

c herself

B ▶ **7.1** Listen again. Circle the correct words to complete the description.

Sarah is [1](**short** / **tall**) like Angela. She has [2](**short** / **long**) brown hair and [3](**wears** / **does not wear**) glasses. Angela thinks Sarah is [4](**unattractive** / **attractive**) and has a(n) [5](**friendly** / **unfriendly**) personality.

COMMUNICATION Talking about family

A Circle the correct words to complete the sentences.

1 My personality is (**just like** / **totally different from**) my sister's. We're both friendly and talkative.

2 She looks (**exactly like** / **really different from**) her brother. She's blonde and tall, while he's short with brown hair.

3 My dad is (**not very** / **extremely**) funny. His jokes make us laugh really hard!

4 (**Neither of us** / **Both of us**) are very tall. We're the shortest in our class.

B Answer the questions using your own words.

1 What does your best friend look like?

____

____

2 Who do you look like, your mother or your father? How are you similar?

____

____

7B

LANGUAGE FOCUS Describing appearance and personality

A Circle the correct sentence in each pair.

1 a She says too she's short. b She says she's too short.

2 a He's not all funny. b He's not funny at all.

3 a I think I'm not enough attractive. b I think I'm not attractive enough.

4 a I guess we're kind of shy. b I guess we're kind shy of.

5 a My mom's pretty easygoing. b My mom's easygoing pretty.

B Do the sentences in the first and second columns have the same or different meanings? Write **S** for same or **D** for different.

	First sentence	Second sentence	Same (S) / Different (D)
1	We're not old enough.	We're too old.	
2	My hair's pretty short.	My hair's fairly short.	
3	He's extremely unfriendly.	He's not friendly at all.	
4	My friend's not very talkative.	My friend talks a lot.	

C ▶ **7.2** Listen to someone describing a friend. Circle the best answers.

1 What's Steve's personality like?

a He's quiet. **b** He talks a lot.

2 What does Steve look like?

a He's pretty short. **b** He's very short.

3 Steve is quite ______.

a boring to be with **b** fun to be with

LISTENING FOCUS Contracted and uncontracted forms

A ▶ **7.3** Contractions are very common in speech, but we often use the uncontracted form for emphasis. Listen and repeat what you hear.

She's quite shy. ⟶ **She is** really nice, though.
contraction — uncontracted form

We're going to the party tomorrow? ⟶ Yes, **we are** going to the party.
contraction — uncontracted form

B ▶ **7.4** Listen to the sentences. Circle the form the speaker uses.

1 a I am **b** I'm

2 a it is **b** it's

3 a we are **b** we're

4 a is not **b** isn't

5 a he is **b** he's

C ▶ **7.5** Circle the words in **bold** that you think should be contracted. Think about the context of the sentences. Then listen and check.

A: Oh, hello... Um, **I am** the new part-time assistant.

B: Oh, great! You must be Paul. Let me show you where **you will** be working. Is this your first job?

A: Yes, **it is**. This is a really exciting day for me.

B: You look a little nervous!

A: Yeah, **I am** quite nervous!

B: Oh, **do not** worry. Everything will be fine. Let me know if I can help.

A: Thanks, **I will**.

7C

READING

Read the passage and answer the questions below.

Amy Cuddy demonstrating the power pose, a technique she says can help boost a person's self-confidence.

1 Some people are born confident and others aren't, right? Perhaps not. Psychologist Amy Cuddy thinks that we can become more confident simply by changing our body language.

2 Studies have shown that our body language—how we sit, stand, and move around—has an important effect on how other people view us. For example, if you cross your arms and look away, people will probably think you're not interested in what's going on. According to Cuddy, your pose can also affect how confident you feel. If you avoid eye contact and hunch your back, you'll feel less confident.

3 So, how can you increase your self-confidence? One way is by doing what Cuddy calls "the power pose." Stand up straight, legs apart, with your hands on your hips, and hold this pose for two minutes whenever you need a confidence boost. Afterward, you should feel much more confident. Power posing is especially useful before job interviews, for public speaking, or if you're trying to make a sale.

4 Changing our body language isn't very hard to do, and there are many benefits that come with it. Improving your body language can help boost your self-confidence and give other people a good impression of you.

A Match each paragraph to its key idea.

1 Paragraph 1 ○	○ **a** Improving your body language can help you in many ways.
2 Paragraph 2 ○	○ **b** Body language affects how people view you.
3 Paragraph 3 ○	○ **c** Amy Cuddy believes a power pose helps boost a person's confidence.
4 Paragraph 4 ○	○ **d** According to a psychologist, there is a link between confidence and body language.

B Circle the correct answer.

1 What is "body language"?

a A way to communicate how you feel, without using words.

b A technique to boost a person's confidence.

2 Which is a benefit of having good body language?

a People will have a good impression of you. **b** Your health will improve.

3 Which of these techniques is more likely to boost your self-confidence?

a Tap your toes repeatedly when listening to someone speak.

b Stand up straight with your hands on your hips for two minutes.

LISTENING

A ▶ **7.6** Listen. Circle the correct words to complete the summary.

The speaker talks about how to prepare for a [1](**job interview** / **meeting**) and gives several tips on how to feel more [2](**successful** / **confident**) before one. She also talks about ways to improve your [3](**body image** / **body language**).

B ▶ **7.6** Listen again. What advice does the speaker give? Circle the best answer.

1 Remember to ________ when leaving the interview room.

a look serious **b** smile

2 Lean ________ slightly to show you're interested in what the person is saying.

a forward **b** backward

3 You ________ move your hands around as you speak.

a shouldn't **b** can

C **CRITICAL THINKING** Check [✓] each statement that the speaker and Amy Cuddy would probably agree with.

1 Power posing makes you feel more confident. ☐

2 You should use a power pose during a job interview. ☐

3 Body language can affect your confidence. ☐

4 A power pose makes people like you more. ☐

VOCABULARY BUILDING

A Complete the sentences using the words in the box.

avoid	issue	properly	self-esteem	withdraw

1 He was so upset with his classmates that he started to ____________________ from class activities.

2 She has high ____________________ because she believes in herself.

3 Low confidence is a big ____________________ for many students.

4 If you pronounce words ____________________ and clearly, people will understand you better.

5 I exercise regularly to ____________________ gaining weight.

B Read the passage. Then complete the sentences using the words in **bold**.

I think my friend suffers from **self-doubt**. For example, she thinks that she's not very clever, but the truth is that she's really smart. I gave her a **self-help** book to read, and it seems to be helping. I want her to be more **self-confident** and realize how wonderful she is!

1 ____________________ means trying to improve yourself, or solve your own problems.

2 The belief that you aren't good enough is called ____________________.

3 If you are ____________________, you believe in your abilities and value.

7D

TED PLAYLIST

Megan Washington sings as a form of therapy to overcome her stuttering.

WHY I LIVE IN MORTAL DREAD OF PUBLIC SPEAKING

Megan Washington can't stand speaking in public because she stutters—she has trouble saying certain sounds in English. For example, she might say "m-m-m-my name is Megan." In this very personal talk, the singer reveals how she overcomes her fear and avoids stuttering with special techniques.

HOW I BEAT STAGE FRIGHT

When Joe Kowan sings in front of an audience, his hands shake, his heart beats very fast, and he starts sweating a lot. He decided the best way to overcome his problem was to write a song about it. He talks about how he turned his problem into something that brought him success.

YOUR BODY LANGUAGE SHAPES WHO YOU ARE

In this talk, psychologist Amy Cuddy shows us how to do her famous "power pose." According to Cuddy, just two minutes of doing this will make you feel more confident, comfortable, and powerful. She explains the science behind her ideas and shows some interesting examples of body language.

A Which statement best describes all three speakers?

a They all share techniques to be more confident.

b They all have a technique to perform better on stage.

c They all have a fear of speaking in public.

B Check [✓] the correct speaker(s).

1 Who sings as a way to cope with their fears?

☐ Megan Washington ☐ Joe Kowan ☐ Amy Cuddy

2 Which speaker's problem was also the reason for their success?

☐ Megan Washington ☐ Joe Kowan ☐ Amy Cuddy

C Complete each sentence using the correct word from the box.

beat	reveal	technique

1 A ________________ is a particular way of doing something.

2 If you ________________ something, you successfully overcome it.

3 If you ________________ something, you show it so that other people can see it.

D Decide which talk you most want to watch. Watch it online at www.ted.com.

7E

WRITING Describing someone

A Read the sample passage describing someone.

Write two paragraphs. In the first paragraph, say who this person is and describe their appearance.

In the second paragraph, describe the person's personality.

My cousin's name is Sandy. She's very tall, and she has long, black hair. She also has dark skin and eyes. Sandy thinks she's not pretty enough, but I think she's beautiful.

She has a wonderful personality. She's very smart, so she always passes her exams. She's also confident and extremely talkative. She once talked for five minutes before realizing that her phone was switched off! The thing I like most about Sandy is that she's always honest with me.

Use some new words from this unit.

Remember to use *really, not very, not ... enough,* etc.

Give an example of this person's behavior and say what you like most about them.

B Write a description of someone you know. Answer the questions to plan your passage.

1 Who is the person you're going to describe?

2 What do they look like?

3 What is their personality like?

4 What is an example of their typical behavior?

C Now write your passage. Then complete the checklist below.

- ☐ Did you use correct spelling and punctuation?
- ☐ Did you describe the person's appearance and personality?
- ☐ Did you use some new words from this unit?
- ☐ Did you use *really, not very, not ... enough*, etc., correctly?

8 Wild Places

8A

VOCABULARY Natural features

A Match each word to its definition.

1 beach	○	○ **a**	land that has very little water and very few plants
2 canyon	○	○ **b**	a raised part of Earth's surface, larger than a hill
3 desert	○	○ **c**	land that is completely surrounded by water
4 island	○	○ **d**	a sandy area beside a sea or lake
5 lake	○	○ **e**	the water that covers most of Earth's surface
6 mountain	○	○ **f**	a place where a river falls from a high place
7 ocean	○	○ **g**	a deep valley with steep sides
8 waterfall	○	○ **h**	an area of water that is surrounded by land

B Circle the correct words to complete the questions.

1 **A:** How (**deep** / **wide**) is the Grand Canyon?
B: It's over 1,800 meters from the top to the bottom.

2 **A:** How (**high** / **long**) is Mount Kilimanjaro?
B: It's 5,895 meters above sea level.

3 **A:** How (**old** / **wide**) is Lake Superior in Canada?
B: It's about 260 kilometers from one side to the other.

4 **A:** How (**high** / **long**) is the Great Wall of China?
B: It's over 8,800 kilometers from one end to the other.

5 **A:** Why is the Mojave Desert so (**deep** / **dry**)?
B: It gets very little rain, about 17 centimeters a year.

LISTENING An amazing place

▶ **8.1** Listen. Circle the best answers.

1 What was the speaker's job during his volunteer program?
a to count the number of whales **b** to measure the size of whales

2 What is the problem affecting these whales?
a there isn't enough food in the ocean **b** they eat garbage from the ocean

3 The speaker describes the Indian Ocean's ______.
a size **b** depth

COMMUNICATION Talking about places

A Unscramble the words in **bold** to complete the conversation.

A: So where are you going on vacation?

B: To Venice in Italy. **really** / **about it** / **excited** / **I'm**

1 ____!

A: Wow! I read that **in the world** / **the most** / **Venice is** / **interesting city**

2 ____.

B: **Tuscany** / **is** / **I** / **hear that** / **the most** / **scenic city**. I might visit there, too.

3 ____.

B Answer the questions using your own words.

1 What's the most interesting place to visit in your country? Why?

____

2 What is the most scenic city in your country?

____

8B

LANGUAGE FOCUS Discussing natural wonders

A Find the grammar mistakes in these sentences and correct them.

1 The Pacific Ocean is bigger the Indian Ocean.

2 Mount Everest is the more famous mountain in the world.

3 I think Australia's beaches are most nice than Europe's beaches.

B You want to go on a city vacation, so you are researching cities to visit. Look at the facts about three cities and answer the questions on page 57.

	Mexico City	Taipei	Vancouver
Average temperature	18 °C	23 °C	10 °C
Size	1,485 km^2	272 km^2	115 km^2

The city of Vancouver, Canada, as seen from Stanley Park.

1 Which city is warmer, Mexico City or Taipei?

____

2 Which is the coldest city?

____

3 Which city is smaller, Taipei or Vancouver?

____

C ▶ **8.2** Listen. Circle the best answers.

1 Which waterfall is higher?
   a Bridal Veil Falls   **b** Omaru Falls

2 Which was the most crowded beach?
   a Ninety Mile Beach   **b** Hot Water Beach

3 The speaker describes New Zealand as the ______ place she's visited.
   a most beautiful   **b** most interesting

LISTENING FOCUS Reduced speech

A ▶ **8.3** We often make words and phrases shorter when we speak informally. This is called reduced speech. Listen and repeat what you hear.

See you tomorrow! ⟶ **Seeya** tomorrow!
Come on, let's go! ⟶ **C'mon**, let's go!

B ▶ **8.4** Match each phrase to its reduced speech form. Then listen and check your answers.

1 going to ○	○ **a** gotta
2 give me ○	○ **b** getcha
3 got to ○	○ **c** gonna
4 get you ○	○ **d** gimme
5 sort of ○	○ **e** lemme
6 let me ○	○ **f** sorta

C ▶ **8.5** Listen to the sentences. Write out the full form of the words you hear.

1 I'm __________ go to Mexico!

2 __________ guess: You're going with your classmates.

3 I __________ explore some caves there.

4 It's __________ cloudy today.

5 Bye, I've __________ go!

6 Can you __________ a lift to the library?

8C

READING

Read the passage and answer the questions below.

1 In 1990, Ho Khanh, a farmer in Vietnam, accidentally discovered the biggest cave in the world—a cave so big it could fit a 747 airplane in it. Ho was out collecting wood deep in the jungle when he came across the entrance to an enormous cave. The story of this huge cave spread quickly, but not everyone believed Ho.

2 In 2006, several British cave explorers came to Ho's house. They had heard about the cave and wanted him to show it to them. Unfortunately, Ho could not remember where the cave was. Two years later, Ho finally found the giant cave again.

3 The explorers came back, and the team traveled through the jungle to the cave's location. When they went inside, they were amazed at its size. Measuring 200 meters high, 150 meters wide, and over 4 kilometers long—it was the largest cave they had ever seen. Ho named the cave Hang Son Doong, meaning Mountain River Cave.

4 Since then, Ho has been a guide for the team on several other explorations. His new passion is to find other undiscovered caves and show people the hidden wonders in the area.

Hang Son Doong, or Mountain River Cave, is so huge that it has its own river, jungle, and climate.

A What is the passage mainly about?

a a farmer who became a cave explorer

b the discovery of the world's largest cave

c cave explorers who find undiscovered caves in Vietnam

B Match each paragraph to its main idea.

1 Paragraph 1 ○ ○ **a** how the discovery changed Ho's life

2 Paragraph 2 ○ ○ **b** the discovery of the cave

3 Paragraph 3 ○ ○ **c** facts about the cave

4 Paragraph 4 ○ ○ **d** the struggle to find the cave again

LISTENING

A ▶ **8.6** Listen. Choose the best title for the talk.

a Discovering an Ancient City in China

b The Discovery of China's Clay Army

B ▶ **8.6** Listen again. Circle the correct answers.

1 What did the farmers find?

a clay statues

b a very deep well

2 Why was the discovery so amazing?

a It is an important clue to discovering China's history.

b The statues were created with a lot of detail.

3 According to experts, the terracotta army was meant to ________.

a protect the first emperor after his death

b frighten the emperor's enemies

C **CRITICAL THINKING** What do the reading passage and the talk have in common? Circle the best answer.

a They both discuss events that happened in China.

b They are both about discoveries that made a person famous.

c They are both about amazing discoveries that were made by farmers.

VOCABULARY BUILDING

A Complete the sentences using the words in the box.

contrast	landscape	plateau	populated	species

1 A ____________ is a high, flat area of land, for example Table Mountain in South Africa.

2 Asia is a highly ____________ continent—more than 4.4 billion people live there.

3 In Africa, dry deserts ____________ with wet rain forests.

4 The ____________ is everything you can see when you look across an area of land.

5 More than 1,500 ____________ of fish live on Australia's Great Barrier Reef.

B Complete each sentence using a word from the box.

popularity	popularize	population

1 The ____________ of a country, city, or area refers to all the people living there.

2 The ____________ of someone or something is how much they are liked by other people.

3 To ____________ something means to make a lot of people interested in it.

8D

TED PLAYLIST

Pure Imagination Cave, at the Sandy Glacier on Mt. Hood, Oregon, U.S.A.

DEEP UNDER THE EARTH'S SURFACE, DISCOVERING BEAUTY AND SCIENCE

Francesco Sauro travels deep underground to explore caves. He talks about exploring a mountain cave in South America. It's a dangerous place, as a fall or rush of water could hurt him. However, it's also fascinating, with Sauro finding new minerals and insects unlike any others in the world.

MY GLACIER CAVE DISCOVERIES

Eddy Cartaya talks about being the first person to explore caves deep inside a glacier of frozen water. Cartaya made maps of three ice caves inside the Sandy Glacier in Oregon. He talks about the magical colors of the caves, the weird bacteria that live in them, and the fantastic ice shapes he saw.

LIFE IN THE DEEP OCEANS

David Gallo explores the deep oceans with submarines, taking videos of the incredible life and landscapes he finds there. Gallo tells us about 64,000 kilometer-long mountain ranges under the sea and glowing jellyfish that grow up to 46 meters long. Gallo's talk reminds us that the deep ocean is a mysterious world that we barely know.

A Select the best title for the playlist.

a Exploring New Places **b** Exploring the Oceans **c** Discovering Glaciers

B Circle the correct answer.

1 Which speaker observes sea creatures?
a Francesco Sauro **b** Eddy Cartaya **c** David Gallo

2 Which speaker studies rocks and insects?
a Francesco Sauro **b** Eddy Cartaya **c** David Gallo

3 Which speaker goes into ice caves?
a Francesco Sauro **b** Eddy Cartaya **c** David Gallo

C Match each word to its definition.

1 glacier ○ ○ **a** unknown
2 submarine ○ ○ **b** a huge mass of ice which moves very slowly, often down a mountain valley
3 mysterious ○ ○ **c** a type of ship that can move underwater

D Decide which talk you most want to watch. Watch it online at www.ted.com.

8E

WRITING A place I'd like to visit

A Read the sample passage about an interesting place.

Write two paragraphs. In the first paragraph, say what the place is, where it is, and when the best time to visit is.

I'd love to visit Angel Falls in the Canaima National Park in Venezuela. The best time to go is from June to December, when there is lots of water. During the dry season, the river has less water, and it's less impressive.

Include some facts about the place.

In the second paragraph, say why you want to visit and what you would do there.

I want to go there because it's the world's highest waterfall—979 meters from top to bottom. It looks really beautiful. I would take lots of photos and go hiking up the mountains in the area.

Remember to use comparatives or superlatives.

Use some new words from this unit.

B Write about a city you want to visit. Answer the questions to plan your passage.

1 What is the name of the city? Where is it?

2 When is the best time to visit it?

3 Why do you want to visit it?

4 What would you do there?

C Now write your passage. Then complete the checklist below.

- ☐ Did you use correct spelling and punctuation?
- ☐ Did you use some new words from this unit?
- ☐ Did you say why you want to go to the place?
- ☐ Did you use comparatives or superlatives?

9 Achievements

9A

VOCABULARY Personal achievements

A Circle the correct words to complete the sentences.

1 When I (**finish** / **win**) college, I'm going to travel for six months.

2 He wants to get (**into** / **on**) shape before summer vacation.

3 My sister wants to (**climb** / **run**) a marathon.

4 My brother (**passed** / **won**) an award at school.

5 All of my friends (**gave** / **got**) into college.

6 I'm so glad I (**passed** / **won**) my exam.

7 I want to (**make** / **start**) a business selling sports gear.

8 Yesterday, we (**gave** / **spoke**) a presentation about trees.

B Answer the questions using your own words.

1 What was your biggest achievement last year?

____

2 Which of the achievements in **A** would you like to accomplish? Why?

____

____

LISTENING My great achievement

A ▶ **9.1** Listen. Who is the talk about?

a a kindergarten child **b** a cyclist **c** a marathon runner

B ▶ **9.1** Listen again. Complete the timeline of Karnazes' achievements.

- **1974:** On his 12th birthday, he [1](**ran** / **cycled**) 64 kilometers just for fun.
- **2005:** He ran for [2](**50** / **80**) hours without sleeping, covering [3](**100** / **563**) kilometers.
- **2006:** He ran [4](**50** / **80**) marathons in [5](**50** / **100**) days. His achievement [6](**inspired** / **forced**) many people to get active.

COMMUNICATION Talking about an achievement

A Circle the best response.

1 How did the competition go?

a I guess you're really happy. **b** Quite good. I won third place.

2 Did you get a prize?

a Yes, I won a tablet. **b** I'm very pleased.

3 I guess you're delighted!

a Well done! **b** Yes, I am.

B Complete the conversation using your own words.

A: Hey! How did the [1] ____________________ go?

B: Pretty well! I came in first.

A: Oh, [2] ____________________! Did you get a prize?

B: Yeah, the prize money was $100.

A: So, you must feel [3] ____________________.

B: I am! I'm really proud of myself.

9B

LANGUAGE FOCUS Discussing past events

A Complete the information using the correct form of the words in parentheses.

In 1953, Edmund Hillary and Tenzing Norgay [1] ____________ (become) the first people to climb Mount Everest. Hillary was from New Zealand, and Norgay was from Nepal. They [2] ____________ (take) three weeks to climb the mountain but only [3] ____________ (spend) 15 minutes at the top.

B Answer the questions using the information from **A**.

1 Were Hillary and Norgay the first people to climb Everest?

____.

2 Was Edmund Hillary from Nepal?

____.

3 Did Tenzing Norgay climb Mount Everest?

____.

4 Did they spend an hour at the top?

____.

C ▶ **9.2** Listen. Complete the sentences using information from the talk.

1 The speaker ________________ (like) running when she was young.

2 She ________________ (run) a marathon in San Francisco.

3 The training ________________ (is) hard at first.

4 She ________________ (finish) the race in about five hours.

5 Her friend ________________ (finish) the race.

LISTENING FOCUS Past tense

A ▶ **9.3** The past tense form of most verbs ends in *-ed*. There are three ways to pronounce this. Listen and repeat what you hear.

/ɪd/ sound:

We **started** two hours ago because we **wanted** to end early.

/t/ sound:

I **finished** the race in last place and **laughed** loudly.

/d/ sound:

As I **traveled** around the world, I **learned** many languages.

B ▶ **9.4** Listen to the sentences. How does the past tense form sound? Circle the sound you hear.

1 **a** /ɪd/ **b** /t/ **c** /d/

2 **a** /ɪd/ **b** /t/ **c** /d/

3 **a** /ɪd/ **b** /t/ **c** /d/

4 **a** /ɪd/ **b** /t/ **c** /d/

C ▶ **9.5** Write each verb in the correct pronunciation group. Listen and check your answers.

climbed	greeted	hoped	washed
lifted	liked	skied	ended

/ɪd/	/t/	/d/

9C

READING

Read the passage and answer the questions below.

1 Growing up, Lewis Pugh loved to read stories about explorers and dreamed of becoming one. At age 17, a month after his first swimming lesson, he swam seven kilometers in the Atlantic Ocean—just to challenge himself. Pugh later became a lawyer, but he quit his job so that he could become a professional swimmer.

2 In 2006, Pugh became the first person to complete a long-distance swim in all five of the world's oceans. A year later, he headed to the North Pole where he swam for 19 minutes in near freezing waters.

3 In 2010, Pugh faced his most intense challenge yet. He swam across Lake Pumori, which was formed when a glacier melted, on Mount Everest. Not only was the water incredibly cold, but it was the highest swim ever at about 5,300 meters above sea level.

4 Later that year, Pugh wrote a best-seller about his adventures. Not surprisingly, he called it *Achieving the Impossible*.

Pugh swimming in the icy cold waters of Peter I Island, Norway

A Which sentence best describes Lewis Pugh?

a He's one of the fastest swimmers in the world.

b He wants to teach people the benefits of swimming.

c He swims in places that people normally wouldn't.

B Complete the timeline using information from the passage.

1986
When he was 17, Pugh swam seven kilometers in the [1] ____________ because he wanted to challenge himself.

2006
He became the only person to swim long distance in all five of the world's [2] ____________.

2007
He swam for 19 minutes at the [3] ____________.

2010
He swam across a lake 5,300 meters above sea level—the [4] ____________ swim anyone has done. He also wrote a book called [5] ____________.

LISTENING

A ▶ **9.6** Listen. Choose the best title for the talk.

a Lewis Pugh: Why He Swims

b Lewis Pugh: The Early Years

c Lewis Pugh: Swimming Across the Atlantic

B ▶ **9.6** Listen again. Match the sentence halves.

1 Pugh swims in order to ○	○ **a** raise awareness of melting sea ice.
2 He swam in all five oceans to ○	○ **b** draw attention to environmental issues.
3 He swam at the North Pole to ○	○ **c** appeal for protected areas of the oceans.
4 He swam on Mount Everest to ○	○ **d** highlight that the Himalayan glaciers are melting.

C **CRITICAL THINKING** Circle the statement you most agree with. Give a reason for your answer.

a The challenges Lewis Pugh does are a good way of raising awareness.

b These challenges are too dangerous and probably won't make a difference.

c People like Lewis Pugh and Robert Swan inspire others to achieve great things.

Reason: ____

VOCABULARY BUILDING

A Match each word to its definition.

1 beneath ○	○ **a** scary
2 frightening ○	○ **b** change from a solid to a liquid
3 head to ○	○ **c** under
4 intense ○	○ **d** staying alive
5 melt ○	○ **e** go
6 survival ○	○ **f** extreme

B Read the passage. Then match each phrase in **bold** to its meaning.

In 1911, Roald Amundsen and Robert Falcon Scott **went head-to-head** in a competition to reach the South Pole. Members of both teams were cold **from head to toe**. Things **came to a head** with Amundsen's team reaching the South Pole first. Scott's team arrived weeks later, but tragically died on their return journey.

1 go head-to-head ○	○ **a** reach an important point
2 from head to toe ○	○ **b** compete directly
3 come to a head ○	○ **c** affecting your whole body

9D

TED PLAYLIST

Roz Savage preparing to row solo across the Pacific Ocean

In 2005, Roz Savage gave up her career as a management consultant to row across the Atlantic. Her next mission is to be the first woman to row solo across the Pacific. Her goal is to raise awareness about plastic pollution, climate change, and environmental heroism.

At age 64, Diana Nyad achieved her lifelong goal of swimming from Cuba to Florida, a 260-kilometer journey. Nyad describes some of the challenges she faced and how she overcame them. In this inspiring talk, she shares her secret to success—"To achieve your dreams," she says, "you must never give up, whatever age you are."

After he swam the North Pole, Lewis Pugh vowed never to take another cold-water dip. But when he heard of Lake Imja in the Himalayas—created by recent glacial melting—and Lake Pumori, a body of water at an altitude of 5,300 meters on Mt. Everest, he began a journey that would teach him a new way to approach swimming and climate change.

A Match each title to the correct speaker.

1 My Mind-Shifting Everest Swim ○		○ **a** Diana Nyad
2 Why I'm Rowing Across the Pacific ○		○ **b** Lewis Pugh
3 Never, Ever Give Up ○		○ **c** Roz Savage

B Circle the best answer.

1 What do all the speakers have in common?

a they spend a lot of time in the water

b they swim long distances in the ocean

c they all crossed the Pacific Ocean

2 "You can chase your dreams at any age; you're never too old." Which speaker most likely said this?

a Lewis Pugh **b** Diana Nyad **c** Roz Savage

C Complete each sentence using the words in red.

1 A ____________________ is something you've dreamed of doing your whole life.

2 The word ____________________ means to do something by yourself.

3 If something is at a particular ____________________, it is at that height above sea level.

D Decide which talk you most want to watch. Watch it online at www.ted.com.

9E

WRITING A biography

A Read the sample passage about a person who achieved something important.

Write three paragraphs. In the first paragraph, say who the person is and write about their life.	Neil Armstrong was born in Ohio, U.S.A., in 1930. After finishing college, he joined the U.S. Navy as a pilot. In 1962, NASA chose Armstrong to be an astronaut.	Remember to use the past simple tense.
In the second paragraph, say what the person's achievement is. Include some details.	Armstrong was the first person to walk on the moon on July 20, 1969. While they were on the moon, Armstrong and his partner Buzz Aldrin planted a flag and carried out science experiments.	
In the third paragraph, say how the person inspired you.	Neil Armstrong inspires me because he and the other astronauts were so brave. The mission was very dangerous, and some people said it was impossible. Armstrong showed the world that people can achieve great things if they are brave and work hard.	

B Write a short passage about a person's achievement that inspired you. Answer the questions to plan your passage.

1 Who is the person?

2 What is the person's background?

3 What is their achievement?

4 How did the person inspire you?

C Now write your passage. Then complete the checklist below.

- ☐ Did you use correct spelling and punctuation?
- ☐ Did you use some new words from this unit?
- ☐ Did you say what the person's achievement is?
- ☐ Did you use the simple past tense?

10 Creative Cities

10A

VOCABULARY Qualities of a neighborhood

A Read what people say about their neighborhoods. Match each statement to a quality that describes it.

1	"There are too many cars and buses."	**a**	friendly neighbors
2	"People are helpful and easy to talk to."	**b**	affordable housing
3	"It's easy to find a cheap apartment."	**c**	green space
4	"There are many nice parks nearby."	**d**	good nightlife
5	"There's always a train or bus when you need one."	**e**	heavy traffic
6	"This area has lots of clubs, cinemas, and restaurants."	**f**	reliable public transportation

B Answer the questions using your own words.

1 Which qualities does your neighborhood have?

____

____

2 Which do you think is the most important quality for a neighborhood? Why?

____

____

LISTENING The neighborhood where I grew up

A 10.1 Listen. What does the speaker talk about?

a He explains how his neighborhood is changing.

b He describes his ideal neighborhood.

c He compares his old and new neighborhoods.

B 10.1 Listen again. Which of these qualities apply to the old and new neighborhoods? Write **O** for old, **N** for new, or **B** for both.

1 affordable housing ______

2 clean streets ______

3 friendly neighbors ______

4 good nightlife ______

5 green space ______

6 heavy traffic ______

COMMUNICATION Talking about your neighborhood

A Circle the best response.

1 I heard you moved to a new place.

a Yeah, I've got an apartment now. **b** I'll think about it.

2 So what do you like about your new neighborhood?

a My neighbors are friendly. **b** The traffic's terrible!

3 The public transportation's not very reliable.

a Why don't you go to the park? **b** Why don't you buy a car?

B Imagine you're having a conversation with a friend. Complete the conversation using your own words.

A: So, what's good about your neighborhood?

B: 1 ____________________

A: Sounds great! What else do you like about it?

B: 2 ____________________

A: Is there anything you don't like about it?

B: 3 ____________________

10B

LANGUAGE FOCUS Giving advice and making suggestions

A The following suggestions contain mistakes. Write the suggestions correctly.

1 How about find a new place? ____________________

2 Why you don't take the train? ____________________

3 One thing could we do is share an apartment. ____________________

B Write suggestions to the problems using the ideas in the box.

invite them to a party	move into an apartment instead
plant some trees	start a street-cleaning group

1 Houses in my neighborhood are too expensive.

____

2 The streets in my neighborhood are very dirty.

____

3 I don't know any of my neighbors.

____

4 They've cut down so many trees to make space for the new playground.

____

C ▶ **10.2** Read the suggestions (**a–c**). Then listen to Alice, Carlos, and Soo-jin. Match each person's name to the most suitable suggestion for their problem.

1 Alice ○ ○ **a** You could get a place outside the city.

2 Carlos ○ ○ **b** How about finding a cheaper apartment?

3 Soo-jin ○ ○ **c** Why don't you find a new job closer to you?

LISTENING FOCUS Thought groups

A ▶ **10.3** When we speak, we divide words into groups with short pauses between them. Each of these "thought groups" covers one main idea. Listen and repeat what you hear.

Main idea 1		**Main idea 2**		**Main idea 3**
I live in New York	/	because it's so much fun,	/	and the parks are great!
thought group 1		thought group 2		thought group 3

Main idea 1		**Main idea 2**
I wanted to move to Westfield,	/	but the rent was too high.
thought group 1		thought group 2

B ▶ **10.4** Read the sentences and identify where you think the pauses between thought groups are. Then listen and check your answers.

Ten years ago, my family moved to this neighborhood because it was cheap. It had a bit of a crime problem, and it wasn't very safe. In my opinion, things have improved a lot. It's now a really safe neighborhood with clean streets and excellent schools.

C ▶ **10.5** Listen to some sentences. Which words do the pauses follow? Circle the answers.

1 **a** housing
b affordable
c another

2 **a** trying
b neighborhood
c cleaning

3 **a** want
b downtown
c area

4 **a** Sydney
b and
c new

10C

READING

Read the passage and answer the questions below.

A mural done by Groundswell in the city of New York, U.S.A.

1 "Art creates community, and community creates change." This is the idea behind Groundswell—an organization that improves neighborhoods in New York City by painting art over large walls. One of these neighborhoods is Brownsville. The Brownsville residents wanted to end the crime and poverty that their neighborhood was known for. Five big, colorful paintings were made on several walls around the area. The paintings were about local heroes and carried positive messages such as "Hope," "Respect," and "Brownsville Moving Forward."

2 Groundswell's paintings beautify the neighborhoods and inspire residents, but the project's benefits don't stop there. Organizers ask young people to take part and learn new skills. Most of them are aged between 14 and 21 and are from poor families. Many of them were involved in crime and want a chance to change their lives. By working with artists to design and make the paintings, these young people learn to express themselves, earn money, and get work experience. As artist Chris Soria says, "It's about the talents that people don't realize that they have until they do it."

3 Since a group of artists and activists started Groundswell in 1996, the organization has completed about 500 paintings in different locations across the city. Every year, around 1,000 young people create works of art and help renovate buildings in troubled neighborhoods like Brownsville.

A What is the passage mainly about?

a creative ways to end crime **b** inspirational local heroes **c** improving communities with art

B Complete the summary using information from the passage.

Groundswell organizes neighborhood improvement projects in New York City. It creates paintings on large [1] ________________ to make the neighborhoods more beautiful and to [2] ________________ residents. Young people from [3] ________________ families or with criminal backgrounds can work on the projects. They work with [4] ________________ to design and create paintings in their neighborhoods. By taking part, the young people learn how to [5] ________________ while earning money and gaining valuable work experience.

LISTENING

A ▶ **10.6** Listen. Choose the best title for the talk.

a Improving a Neighborhood with Art and Entertainment

b Residents Beat Crime by Singing in the Streets

c Using Art to Decrease Pollution

B ▶ **10.6** Listen again. Circle the correct words to complete the summary.

Downtown Providence was not popular with visitors due to high crime rates, ugly buildings, and [1](**heavy traffic** / **pollution**). Residents started a [2](**competition** / **festival**) to attract visitors to the neighborhood. There were many [3](**cultural activities** / **sports**) for people to enjoy and take part in. Eventually new businesses opened, and more people [4](**left** / **visited**) the area.

C **CRITICAL THINKING** Use the information (**a–e**) to complete the Venn diagram.

a the neighborhood improved

b a project for young people

c the government gave some help

d local people took action

e art made a difference

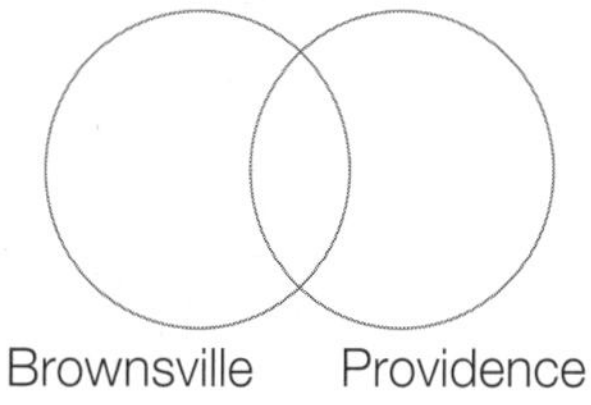

VOCABULARY BUILDING

A Complete the sentences using the words in the box.

block	decline	location	renovate	residents	stage

1 The ____________ are friendly.

2 The apartments on this ____________ are getting more expensive.

3 They were looking for the perfect ____________ for their photoshoot.

4 The museum will ____________ several art exhibitions next month.

5 They decided to ____________ the old buildings in the city.

6 Crime and poverty can cause a neighborhood to ____________.

B Some verbs, such as *renovate*, end with the suffix *-ate*. Complete the sentences using the words in **bold**.

Today I moved to the district of Kreuzberg in Berlin, Germany. It **fascinates** me because it has an amazing mix of cultures. Many young Germans live here because they **appreciate** the fashionable shops and great nightlife. Tonight I'm going to **celebrate** moving here with friends at a restaurant.

1 To ____________ something is to value or admire it.

2 When something ____________ you, you find it extremely interesting.

3 We do something special or fun to ____________ an important event.

Local residents looking at the Before I Die public art display in New Orleans, U.S.A.

TEDTALKS

HOW I BROUGHT A RIVER, AND MY CITY, BACK TO LIFE

It took 20 years, but Aziza Chaouni and her team successfully restored a river in the Moroccan city of Fez. The river was badly polluted and smelly, so no one wanted to go near it. Chaouni explains how her team cleaned the river, making it an attractive place for residents and tourists to hang out.

HOW TO BUILD WITH CLAY ... AND COMMUNITY

After studying architecture in Germany, Diébédo Francis Kéré returned to his village in Burkina Faso to improve life there. His village was very poor and badly needed a school. Kéré taught the residents construction skills, and together they built a school using simple materials like clay and wood.

BEFORE I DIE I WANT TO ...

Candy Chang wrote, "Before I die, I want to ..." on the wall of an abandoned house in New Orleans, U.S.A. Anyone walking by could write whatever they wanted to. Chang says this simple experiment allowed her neighbors to share their thoughts and grow closer to one another.

A The talks are all about ______.

a inspiring change in communities **b** teaching people new skills **c** learning more about communities

B Complete the table using information from the descriptions.

TED Speaker	Where is the neighborhood?	What did the speaker do?	How did it help the residents?
Aziza Chaouni	the city of [1] ______ in Morocco	Along with her team, she cleaned a river.	People started to [2] ______ at the river.
Diébédo Francis Kéré	a [3] ______ in Burkina Faso	He and the villagers [4] ______ using materials like [5] ______.	The residents learned a new skill.
Candy Chang	[6] ______	She conducted an experiment in her neighborhood.	Her [7] ______ wrote down their thoughts. It brought them closer to each other.

C Complete the sentences by circling the correct words.

1 To restore something is to make it (**as it was** / **worse than**) before.

2 Architecture is the art of (**designing** / **demolishing**) buildings.

D Decide which talk you most want to watch. Watch it online at www.ted.com.

10E

WRITING Creative suggestions

A Imagine your town or city wants to renovate a large old building downtown. Read the sample passage about ideas for how to use the building.

Write two paragraphs. Start by saying what your idea is and describe it.

I have an idea for the old building. How about using it as a market? There's no market downtown, so this would be a great opportunity to have one. Local residents could sell things that they make or grow, such as clothes, fruits, and vegetables. It would be a good place for people to buy things, too. It would be open every day. The market would attract people to the area.

Say who would use the building, and why.

Remember to use the suggestion phrases you learned in this unit.

Or, why don't we turn the building into a gym? We could put exercise machines in there and have fitness classes. It would be for local people only and would be open all day. It would help residents stay healthy and help them get to know one another.

B Write a short passage using your ideas. Answer the questions to plan your passage.

1 What is your suggestion?

2 Who would use the building, and how?

3 When would people use it?

4 What are the benefits of your suggestion?

C Now write your passage. Then complete the checklist below.

- ☐ Did you use correct spelling and punctuation?
- ☐ Did you use some new words from this unit?
- ☐ Did you state the benefits of your suggestion?
- ☐ Did you use suggestion phrases from this unit?

11 Picture Perfect

11A

VOCABULARY Photography

A Circle the correct words to complete the sentences.

1 Circles and squares are types of (**colors** / **shapes**).

2 (**Landscape** / **Portrait**) photos normally show the beauty of nature.

3 The flash, lens, and screen are all parts of (**a camera** / **an image**).

4 This photo was so (**boring** / **striking**) that I couldn't get it out of my mind.

5 From this (**background** / **perspective**), the girl looks bigger than the bus!

6 I saw a (**landscape** / **weird**) photo today. It was a picture of an upside-down room!

7 I took a lot of (**paintings** / **pictures**) with my new camera.

B Answer the questions about a photo you know using your own words.

1 What kind of photo is it (e.g., portrait, landscape)? What is the photo of?

____

2 What is your opinion of the photo? Why do you think this?

____

3 What kind of photos do you usually like? Why?

____

LISTENING My perfect photo

A ▶ **11.1** Listen. Where do you think the speakers are?

a at an art gallery **b** at the library **c** at a museum

B ▶ **11.1** Listen again. Complete the summary by circling the correct words.

Photo 1

This is a [1](**landscape** / **wildlife**) photo. The male speaker likes the colors while the female speaker thinks that the use of [2](**light** / **perspective**) is interesting. She thinks the colors are too [3](**weird** / **bright**).

Photo 2

This is a [4](**landscape** / **portrait**) photo. The male speaker thinks the photo is [5](**strange** / **stunning**) and full of happiness. The female speaker likes the fact that there is [6](**a lot of** / **no**) color.

COMMUNICATION Giving your opinion

A Two friends are looking for a photo for their website. Unscramble the sentences to complete the conversation.

A: Hey, (**think of** / **this** / **do you** / **what** / **photo**)?

1 ______________________________

B: Well, in my opinion, it's a little weird.

A: Really? (**I** / **the** / **colors** / **like**).

2 ______________________________

B: It's just a bit too bright for my liking. How about this one?

A: Wow! That's (**the most** / **I've ever** / **stunning shots** / **one of** / **seen**)!

3 ______________________________

B: Let's go with this one then!

B Imagine you're having a conversation with a friend about the photo on page 127 of the Student Book. Complete the conversation using your own words.

A: So, what do you like about the photo?

B: 1 ______________________________

A: Right, that's true. And what don't you like about it?

B: 2 ______________________________

A: Yeah, I think so too. If you could change one thing about it, what would it be?

B: 3 ______________________________

11B

LANGUAGE FOCUS Discussing opinions

A Circle the correct words to complete the conversation.

1 **A:** Do you (**think** / **believe**) this photo looks like a painting?

B: No, I don't. It's obvious it's a photo.

2 **A:** How do you (**find** / **feel**) about this wildlife photo?

B: In my opinion, it's stunning!

3 **A:** Well, your camera (**seems** / **seems like**) fine to me. It's not broken.

B: Are you sure? It (**look** / **looks like**) there's a crack on the screen.

B Answer the questions using your own words.

1 What do you think of photography as a hobby?

___

2 Do you find portraits interesting? Why?

___

3 How do you feel about pictures of baby animals?

___

C ▶ **11.2** Listen. Circle the best response.

1 How does the female speaker feel about the photo?

a She thinks it's beautiful. b She finds it weird.

2 What problem does the male speaker have with the photo?

a He thinks it looks like the ocean. b He thinks the colors are weird.

3 Which speaker thinks that the photo should not be altered?

a male speaker b female speaker

LISTENING FOCUS /d/ sounds

A ▶ **11.3** When we make the /t/ sound between two vowel sounds, it can sound like /d/. Listen and repeat what you hear

That pho**t**o's not very pre**tt**y. Please take i**t** again.

Just take pictures of wha**t**ever seems interesting. That's be**tt**er!

B ▶ **11.4** Circle each word in which the /t/ sound is said like the /d/ sound. Then listen and check your answers.

thought	butter	lot
perspective	letter	math
exciting	listen	writer

C ▶ **11.5** Listen. Complete the sentences with the words you hear.

1 I'm ___ years old now.

2 I've taken a ___ of pictures, thousands.

3 My dad let me use his cheap ___ camera to take a picture of a lake.

4 The ___ looked amazing.

5 It was bright and shining like ___.

11C

READING

Read the passage and answer the questions below.

With the availability of smartphones, anyone can take a photo and upload it to the Internet within seconds.

1 Photography used to be just for the experts, but now we're all photographers. Only 20 years ago, taking a good photo wasn't easy. Cameras were bulky and film was expensive. Photographers would take a photo only if they were sure it was a good shot. Nowadays, everyone has a smartphone with a camera in their pocket, and to capture an image, you just have to tap on a screen. If you want to enhance a photo, you just need to tap a couple of times more.

2 Not only are pictures easy to take, they're also easy to share. Gone are the days of waiting hours for photos to be developed and receiving one print of each image. Instead, amateur photographers can now snap and share their images with the world in seconds by posting them online.

3 Sites such as Instagram host millions of photos of daily life around the world. You can follow a friend's vacation adventures, check out what people around the world are having for breakfast, or view strangers' photos of their pets. These days, anyone can tell their story as it happens.

4 With so many photographs on the Web every day, no one image gets to be special for long. But if there are fewer memorable images today, it's not because there are fewer good images. It's because there are so many of them.

A What is the main idea of the passage? Choose the best answer.

a Nowadays, photos are easy to take and share.

b There are too many photographs nowadays.

c Sharing photos makes life better for everyone.

B Match each paragraph to its main idea.

1 Paragraph 1 ○	○ **a** Good photos don't remain special for long.
2 Paragraph 2 ○	○ **b** People share their stories through their photos.
3 Paragraph 3 ○	○ **c** Taking photos is much easier than it was in the past.
4 Paragraph 4 ○	○ **d** Sharing photos is a simple thing to do.

LISTENING

A ▶ **11.6** Listen. Choose the best title for the talk.

a Photography and Technology **b** Photography: A Dying Art **c** Photographs Around the World

B ▶ **11.6** Listen again. Circle the best answers.

1 Smartphones make photos ______.

a more beautiful **b** less special **c** more artistic

2 Around ______ photos are uploaded to the Internet every day.

a two thousand **b** two million **c** two billion

3 It's difficult to see a really good photo online because ______.

a most photos are terrible **b** people don't upload them **c** there are too many photos

C **CRITICAL THINKING** Circle the statement you most agree with. Give a reason for your answer.

a Taking photos is easier than before.

b Photographs are getting better due to new technology.

c Everyone can be a photographer nowadays.

Reason: ______________________________

VOCABULARY BUILDING

A Answer the questions using the words in the box.

amateur	**enhance**	**capture**	**dawn**	**shadow**

1 What forms behind an object when light hits it? ______________

2 Which word means "take a photo" or "record"? ______________

3 What's the opposite of "professional"? ______________

4 Which word means "to improve"? ______________

5 What's another way of saying "sunrise"? ______________

B Complete the sentences using the phrases in **bold**.

- **From the dawn of time**, people have been fascinated by animals.
- It **dawned on** him that he should pursue his passion instead of being stuck in a boring job.
- It isn't easy; he often works **from dawn till dusk**.

1 ______________________ means "realized something for the first time."

2 If something lasts ______________________, it lasts all day.

3 ______________________ is another way of saying "for a very long time."

11D

TED PLAYLIST

Flying drones with cameras are used to take photos of inaccessible places.

THIS NEW TELESCOPE MIGHT SHOW US THE BEGINNING OF THE UNIVERSE

Wendy Freedman talks about photographing space: how to do it, what we can learn, and what the future holds. Freedman's team is building the world's largest telescope, which will be able to take incredible pictures of space when it's finished in 2025.

DIVE INTO AN OCEAN PHOTOGRAPHER'S WORLD

Thomas Peschak shares his love of the underwater world with us, describing his many years of adventures as an ocean photographer. He shows us magnificent photos of fish, whales, and seals and highlights the danger of losing our marine wildlife forever.

A FLYING CAMERA ... ON A LEASH

By flying high up above cities, ancient sites, and natural places, drones can give us a new perspective on familiar things. Sergei Lupashin talks about this and the other opportunities that flying machines offer photographers.

A The playlist is about photography that ______.

a makes us laugh **b** captures stunning events **c** helps us learn new things

B Use the information (**a–e**) to complete the Venn diagram.

a uses new technology to take photos
b takes photos underwater
c talks about photography
d uses a flying machine
e takes photos of space

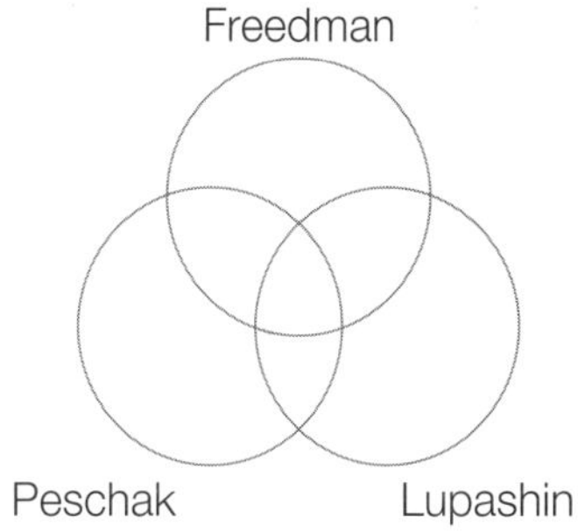

C Circle the correct words to complete the sentences.

1 If something is magnificent, it is (**impressive** / **big**).
2 A marine animal lives (**in the ocean** / **underground**).
3 An opportunity (**allows** / **forces**) you to do something you (**want** / **don't want**) to do.

D Decide which talk you most want to watch. Watch it online at www.ted.com.

11E

WRITING Describing a photo

A Read the sample passage of someone describing a photo.

Write two paragraphs. In the first paragraph, say what the photo is of and where you found it. Say what type of photo it is and how it makes you feel.

I love this photo of a street in Tokyo that I found online. It's a street full of people and it looks really busy. It's a landscape photo, but it's not of nature. The photo makes me feel like I'm going out for the evening in a lively place.

Remember to use the sense verbs you learned in this unit.

In the second paragraph, say what you like and dislike about the photo.

I really like the perspective because the shot is taken from high up. The only thing I don't like about it is that some of the people are blurred because they're moving.

Use some new words from this unit.

B Write a description of a photo you really like. Answer the questions to plan your passage.

1 What is the photo of? Where did you find it?

2 How does the photo make you feel?

3 What do you like about the photo?

4 What don't you like about the photo?

C Now write your passage. Then complete the checklist below.

- ☐ Did you use correct spelling and punctuation?
- ☐ Did you say what you like about the photo?
- ☐ Did you use some new words from this unit?
- ☐ Did you use some sense verbs from this unit?

12 Healthy Habits

12A

VOCABULARY Habits

A Circle the correct words to complete the sentences.

1 I want to stay healthy so I (**take** / **use**) vitamins daily and (**eat** / **use**) a balanced diet.

2 I usually (**eat** / **drink**) fruit juice and (**eat** / **take**) vegetables for lunch.

3 If you (**eat** / **take**) fruit every day and (**get** / **take**) some exercise, you'll soon feel healthier.

4 When I (**get** / **take**) less than eight hours of sleep, I feel tired all day.

5 You should always (**brush** / **wash**) your hands before eating.

6 It's important to (**do** / **have**) exercise if you want to keep fit.

7 I'm trying to (**eat** / **drink**) healthier so I (**avoid** / **use**) red meat.

8 He (**brushes** / **does**) his teeth and (**drinks** / **uses**) mouthwash after having a meal.

B Answer the questions using the words in **A**.

1 What two things do you do to keep healthy?

____

____

2 Do you think your diet is generally healthy or unhealthy? Why or why not?

____

____

LISTENING My healthy (and unhealthy) habits

A ▶ 12.1 Circle the best answer.

1 What is the best title for the talk?

- **a** Technology and Exercise
- **b** The Best Fitness Apps
- **c** Exercise Tips for Busy People

2 According to the speaker, a person who doesn't want to carry a smartphone while exercising should probably get a(n) ________.

- **a** exercise app
- **b** fitness tracker
- **c** smartwatch

B ▶ **12.1** Listen again. Complete the summary using words from the talk.

	Advantages	Disadvantages
Exercise apps	• Tracks your progress • Can replace a [1] ________	• Need to carry a [2] ________ —quite large and can break easily.
[3] ________	• Counts your steps • Tells you how much energy you've burned. • Fairly cheap	• Only useful if you [4] ________
Smartwatch	• Does everything a [5] ________ does, but also uses [6] ________ like a smartphone	• Pretty expensive • Batteries don't last a long time.

COMMUNICATION Talking about healthy options

A Circle the best response.

1 I read that drinking too much water can be dangerous for your health.

a That's interesting to know. **b** I'm not sure.

2 Why do you exercise?

a Twice a day. **b** When I do, I feel really good.

3 I drink a can of soda every day.

a Apparently, that's bad for you. **b** I don't agree.

B Replace the words in **bold** using words from the box.

apparently	if	good for you	how come

A: **Someone told me that** you should eat five pieces of fruit a day. [1] ________

B: Oh, really? **What's the reason**? [2] ________

A: Well, it's **very healthy**. [3] ________

B: Sure, but why five pieces?

A: Experts say that **when** you eat five pieces, you get all the fiber and vitamins you need for one day. [4] ________

12B

LANGUAGE FOCUS Discussing healthy habits

A Circle the correct word to complete each sentence.

1 When I (**ate** / **eat**) red meat, I feel unwell the next day.

2 If someone (**avoided** / **avoids**) sugar, their teeth are healthier.

3 Whenever I (**drink** / **drank**) tea, I sleep very well at night.

B Match each cause to its effect. Then write sentences with them. The first one is given.

use mouthwash ○	○ gain weight
sleep well ○	○ heart rate increases
eat unhealthy food ○	○ teeth become healthier
exercise ○	○ feel less tired

1 When you use mouthwash, your teeth become healthier.

2 ______________________________

3 ______________________________

4 ______________________________

C ▶ **12.2** Listen. Circle the best answer.

1 What is the conversation about?
   a how to lose weight **b** how to burn energy at night

2 Why shouldn't you eat late at night?
   a Your body doesn't use the energy because you're sleeping.
   b Your body burns too much energy at night.

3 Why should you never skip breakfast?
   a You'll burn more energy. **b** You won't feel so hungry later in the day.

4 What should you do if you want to eat less during a meal?
   a drink a glass of water **b** don't eat too late

LISTENING FOCUS Linking words

A ▶ **12.3** When we speak, we sometimes join words together. This is called *linking*. We link words that end with consonant sounds to words that start with vowel sounds. Listen and repeat what you hear.

A: Soda contains loads‿of sugar. You should‿order something‿else.

B: Well, how‿about juice? Or does‿it contain sugar, too?

B ▶ **12.4** Underline the words that should be linked. Then listen and check your answers.

1 An exercise buddy can make working out more fun.

2 You should always wash your hands before meals.

3 You can easily gain weight if you eat late-night snacks.

C ▶ **12.5** Listen. Complete the paragraph using words from the talk.

My [1]______________ brushes her teeth just after eating, as she [2]______________ makes her mouth feel cleaner. [3]______________ actually a mistake. Your mouth is acidic after a meal and brushing immediately after can damage your teeth. Instead, wait 30 [4]______________ eating before brushing your teeth.

12C

READING

Read the passage and answer the questions below.

1 "Look after your teeth if you don't want to lose them!" Parents often give this advice to their children, but not many take it seriously. One common way that people damage their teeth is by drinking sugary drinks, such as soda. The sugar in the drink coats the teeth, and bacteria then turn the sugar into acid. The acid softens teeth and causes stubborn stains.

2 After people have finished their soda, they frequently start chewing on the ice. This is also bad news for teeth. Crunching ice or other hard foods can cause tiny cracks in teeth, making them weak and painful. Worse, there are some foods that are both hard and sugary, such as hard candy. It's sticky, too, so it's hard to remove it from teeth.

3 So, you might think, I'll just brush harder to remove the sugar, right? Wrong. Brushing hard or using a hard toothbrush also damages your teeth. You can easily scratch your teeth—even though they might seem rock-solid. So, to keep your teeth healthy, avoid these bad habits!

To prevent sugar in sweet drinks from coating your teeth, use a straw.

A Choose the best title for the passage.

a Habits that Harm Your Teeth **b** Good Brushing Habits **c** Sugar: What You Need to Know

B Complete the chart using words from the passage.

Causes		Results
[1] ______ turn sugar from sodas into acid.	→	The acid then [2] ______ our teeth and causes stains.
People chew on [3] ______ food like ice.	→	This can cause tiny [4] ______ in our teeth.
Using a [5] ______ toothbrush to brush teeth.	→	This can [6] ______ our teeth.

LISTENING

A ▶ **12.6** Listen. Choose the best title for the talk.

a Cleaning Your Teeth Properly

b Foods that Strengthen Teeth

c Protecting Your Teeth

B ▶ **12.6** Listen again. Circle the correct word to complete each sentence.

1 Instead of consuming (**candy** / **sugary drinks**), have some (**cheese** / **fruit**).

2 Eating some (**cheese** / **fruit**) after having something sugary reduces acid levels in your mouth.

3 Brush your teeth (**gently** / **quickly**) with a soft toothbrush and use mouthwash.

4 Eat a (**low-fat** / **varied**) diet to keep your teeth healthy.

C **CRITICAL THINKING** Circle the statement you most agree with. Give a reason for your answer.

a Teeth don't need much care—just brush twice a day.

b Stores should stop selling sugary foods and drinks.

c Kids should have fruit instead of candy to save their teeth.

Reason: ____

VOCABULARY BUILDING

A Match each word in the box to its definition.

frequently	global	prevent	spread	vital

1 to stop something from happening ______________

2 affecting the whole world ______________

3 often ______________

4 to reach a larger area ______________

5 important ______________

B Complete the sentences using the words in the box.

global	globalization	globe

1 Many people are worried about environmental changes caused by ______________ warming.

2 A ______________ is a round object with a map of the world on it.

3 ______________ has made it easier for goods and people to be transported around the world.

TEDTALKS

12D

TED PLAYLIST

Matt Cutts offers practical advice on setting and achieving goals.

WHY DIETING DOESN'T USUALLY WORK

Dieting doesn't work and might make you fatter. That's Sandra Aamodt's belief, and she should know. Not only did she diet for 30 years, but she's also studied dieting as a scientist. Aamodt says to lose weight, you must change your eating habits. And the rules are simple—eat when you're hungry, and stop when you're full.

TRY SOMETHING NEW FOR 30 DAYS

New hobbies or habits can be time-consuming, so why not try one for just 30 days? Matt Cutts did this, starting with small habits, like cycling to work or taking a photo every day. When these succeeded, he started adopting more challenging habits, having fun and learning new skills along the way.

A SIMPLE WAY TO BREAK A BAD HABIT

Breaking bad habits could be much easier than you think, Dr. Judson Brewer explains. Instead of forcing yourself to stop the habits, you question them: "Why am I eating this sugary snack?" or "Is stressing about work actually helpful?" By thinking carefully about our bad habits, we make them less powerful.

A What is the playlist about?

- **a** how good habits can help us lose weight
- **b** how to pick up good habits and break bad ones
- **c** how we can get into the habit of regular exercise

B Circle the correct words to complete the summary.

Sandra Aamodt is a scientist. Her talk is about changing [1](**eating** / **exercise**) habits, rather than all habits. Matt Cutts's talk is more about [2](**old** / **new**) habits. He talks about habits he has tried for a [3](**long** / **short**) time. Judson Brewer advises us to [4](**force ourselves to stop** / **think carefully about**) bad habits. All three talks offer practical advice on what to do about our [5](**habits** / **health**) to improve our [6](**careers** / **lives**).

C Match each word in red to its definition.

1. doing or trying something ____________
2. eating less to lose weight ____________
3. instructions that tell you what you must or must not do ____________

D Decide which talk you most want to watch. Watch it online at www.ted.com.

12E

WRITING Health tips

A Read the sample passage about how to avoid spreading the flu.

Write three paragraphs. In the first paragraph, write a brief introduction and give your first tip.

In each paragraph, say what the tip is and how it helps avoid spreading the disease.

Here are three tips to help you avoid spreading the flu. First, when you have the flu, don't go to school or work. If you go to places that are full of people, you pass on the disease. Stay home instead.

Second, if you're around people with the flu, wear a mask and don't touch your eyes, nose, or mouth. You can pick up germs with your hands, and when you touch these places, the flu germs enter your body. Wash your hands first.

Third, keep your surroundings clean. For example, clean door handles and light switches regularly. Sick people could leave their germs in these places and spread the flu.

Remember to give reasons.

Use some new words from this unit.

B Choose a disease you know about. Write a short passage on how to avoid spreading this disease. Answer the questions to plan your passage.

1 What is the disease you have chosen? What is your first tip? How does it prevent the disease from spreading?

2 What is your second tip? How does it prevent the disease from spreading?

3 What is your third tip? How does it prevent the disease from spreading?

C Now write your passage. Then complete the checklist below.

- ☐ Did you use correct spelling and punctuation?
- ☐ Did you use some new words from this unit?
- ☐ Did you explain what disease it is?
- ☐ Did you give three tips, and say how they prevent spreading of the disease?

Audio Scripts

1.1 The last movie I watched was about a famous chef who owns a really nice restaurant. However, he's rude to his customers and starts losing their business. Eventually, his restaurant closes down. He becomes depressed and is really unhappy. Then one day, he stops for food at a small diner next to a highway—the kind of place where you can get a cheap meal. He thinks the food is amazing, and wants to meet the chef. He hopes he might persuade the person to join him in opening a new restaurant. It turns out the chef is a woman who knows who he is and doesn't want anything to do with him. At first they argue a lot, and that's where the movie becomes funny. They throw food at each other and shout—it's really hilarious. However, they soon become friends and then they fall in love. They open a new restaurant together and it's a real success. It was a pretty good movie overall. The movie didn't have many plot twists, but it was entertaining.

1.2 **1.** Do you like Spanish movies?; **2.** Does your brother like this song?; **3.** What's your favorite movie?; **4.** Do your friends like action movies?

1.3 Yes, you're right! I do like rap music.; My mom and dad don't like pop music.; That isn't a romantic comedy. It's an action movie.

1.4 **1.** doesn't; **2.** isn't; **3.** we're

1.5 The kora is a stringed instrument from West Africa. It's a beautiful instrument, big and round at one end, with a long, thin neck at the top. It looks a bit like a lollipop that's half-eaten. Koras have 21 strings, which is a lot—a guitar only has six strings.

Koras are still made in the traditional way, and using traditional materials. The large, round part is made from a big, round vegetable. The vegetable is cut in half and the insides are removed. Then a piece of cow skin is put across the hole. The neck is made from wood.

Koras make lovely music. The sounds are very light and gentle. Kora players sit down to play and use both hands to pluck the strings. Good players can play very quickly, making five or six sounds every second.

2.1

M: Oh, dear! I never seem to have any money!

W: Well, that's probably because you spend it all on clothes!

M: Well, yes, I suppose I do spend a lot on clothes. What about you? How much did that jacket cost?

W: This one? Oh, it was only $50.

M: That's not too bad. I spent the same amount on this shirt.

W: Wow, your shirt cost $50? I'd say that's too much. You should be more careful with your money.

M: I try to be most of the time. Take these shoes, for example. I only paid $15 for these. They were on sale.

W: Well done! They're nice shoes. I also went to a sale recently, and I got these new pants. What do you think?

M: Yeah, they're nice. I love the color. What did they cost? $40?

W: Nope. Get this—they were just $25.

M: $25! I'm impressed! You have to tell me the name of the shop. I'll buy a pair for my sister.

2.2 Hi there! Thank you for agreeing to help with the survey. There are just four questions to answer. Okay, the first question is: Do you ever shop online?

Great! Right, let's move on to question 2. How often do you go to a shopping mall?

Have you got that? Okay. Now, here's the third question: Do you ever buy CDs?

Good. And now the last question: How often do you go shopping with your family?

That's all. Thanks for helping me out!

2.3 coffee, music, makeup / believe, decide, suggest

2.4 One-syllable words: buy, gas, mall, pay, shop; Two-syllable words: habit, money, outfit, shopping, spending

2.5 **1.** I came to col<u>lect</u> my money.; **2.** You got a <u>hair</u>cut.; **3.** We watched a <u>mo</u>vie.; **4.** Let's dis<u>cuss</u> the problem.; **5.** Do you like <u>con</u>certs?; **6.** I be<u>gin</u> work at 9:00 a.m.

2.6 In many countries, there are days or months when some people decide to stop shopping. For example, there is Buy Nothing New Month, which started in 2010, and now some people have started Buy Nothing New Year. These people say they want to spend less money and save the environment.

In my opinion, though, these people are wrong. Not going shopping for a year is a really bad idea. Think about it: if there aren't many customers, we won't need people to work in shops. These people will lose their jobs. Then there are the people who make the products. If people don't buy the products, we won't need people to work in factories, or the people who deliver products to shops in trucks. Millions of people would lose their jobs.

On the whole, businesses would be affected. Thousands of companies would probably close because they wouldn't have any income. If people don't have jobs and companies close, the government would get less tax and there would be less money to spend on improving roads, hospitals and schools. The economy would suffer.

In summary, although there may be some benefits to not shopping, I think there are many more drawbacks. There's no need to give up shopping. Instead, people should focus on careful planning and spending.

3.1 Well, I work in a restaurant with 10 other people. So what do I do every day? Mostly, I look after the other staff, I make sure that they do their jobs. I also talk to the customers in the restaurant, and make sure they're all happy. I guess I don't like the hours, because they're long. I work from 10 a.m. to 10 p.m. And, this job is hard work, because I'm always busy. What I like is the pay! It's good. Also, I like the people, both the staff and the customers. Overall, I'd say it's a pretty good job.

3.2 **1.** What don't you like about your job?; **2.** Do you have a job?; **3.** What's your job like?; **4.** What do you do?

3.3 Do you have a job?; Do you like your job?; What job would you like to have?; What don't you like about your job?

3.4 **1.** Do you have a job?; **2.** Oh, great. So what do you do?; **3.** Mm, that's interesting. Do you like your job?; **4.** So, what don't you like about your job?

3.5 **1.** Do you enjoy your job?; **2.** Do you have a job?; **3.** So what do you do?

3.6 It's important to follow your dreams, but changing your job can be very difficult. Here are some tips to make it easier.

First, don't quit your current job. That's not a good idea! Keep working and look for a new job at the same time. Then you'll have enough money, plus you can change your mind later if you decide not to take the new job.

Second, ask family and friends for advice. They might have some useful tips to help you. They can also let you know if changing jobs is a bad idea. Remember, you don't always know best!

Third, find out as much as you can about the job you want. Talk to people who do this job, or try to read about it online. You could even try doing the job part-time, say for one morning a week.

Finally, don't give up! Keep trying. You'll eventually find the job of your dreams.

4.1 Daniel Tammet has a unique ability. He can remember tens of thousands of numbers. In fact, in 2004, he set a record for being able to recite a 22,000-digit number from memory in just over five hours. He is also able to learn languages very quickly. He knows ten different languages, and says he learned to speak Icelandic in just one week. By comparison, most people take about three months to learn a language.

It's difficult to understand how Tammet learns so quickly. He says that every word and number has its own shape, color, and feeling in his mind. This makes it easier for him to group them together and remember things.

Tammet has written three books to help other people improve their memories. He has also created a website to help people learn languages the way he does. He's keen to share his amazing gift with others.

4.2

M: Hi! Are you also signing up for Spanish lessons?

W: No, I'm quite fluent in Spanish. How come you're taking lessons?

M: I'm hoping to travel to South America during the summer break. I'd like to be able to talk to the locals in their own language.

W: That sounds fun! I'm actually here to sign up for guitar lessons.

M: Wow! I'd like to hear you play sometime.

W: Actually, I'm not very good. I'm hoping some lessons will help me get better at it.

4.3 sit / seat; see / she; disk / desk

4.4 **1.** ship / sheep; **2.** bat / bet; **3.** sat / set; **4.** pan / pen; **5.** fit / feat; **6.** bin / been

4.5 **1.** Don't forget to **set** your alarm so you'll wake up on time.; **2.** Use a blue **pen** to fill in the form.; **3.** I prefer to **send** emails instead of text messages.; **4.** Be careful! You might **slip** on the ice.; **5.** Have you got a baseball **bat**?; **6.** Can you count the **sheep**?

4.6 Hello, and welcome to *Life Questions*, the podcast that helps you live life to the fullest. This week, I'm going to talk about making your hobby work for you.

Well, there are three main ways to go about it. The first one is sharing what you do on the Internet. Let's say you're really good at skateboarding. You could write a blog about your hobby, or upload photos or videos. If people want to put advertisements on your blog, you can make money by charging a fee.

The second way involves teaching people how to do your hobby. People are always looking for new activities to try, and if you can explain your hobby clearly, it could become your job. For example, if you're really into making clothes, you could run classes or start a website to help people learn.

The last method involves making a product using your hobby and selling it. So if you're really good at playing the guitar, you could sell your music online. Or if you love gardening, you could grow plants and sell them.

Well folks, that's it for today, but keep thinking about different ways you could turn a hobby into paid work. And let us know if you manage to do it! Bye for now!

5.1 I was recently asked to try out a new smart TV—the TruView 2000. It's the latest TV in the range. It's a really fun TV, because you can connect it to the Internet. That means you can visit your favorite websites and watch YouTube videos on it. The display is very clear and it comes with a built-in sound system. Watching movies on this TV is a great experience—it feels like you're in the cinema! Another positive is that it's really thin. Although it measures 100 centimeters across, it's only 3 centimeters thick—which makes it look very modern.

It's a nice TV but it costs $800 and in my opinion, that's too expensive. Other smart TVs with the same functions cost much less. It's also difficult to use. The menus are really confusing. Another problem is that despite being so thin, the TruView 2000 is really heavy. Moving it around to set it up was not easy!

Overall, I give this TV a three out of five.

5.2 **1.** What does your smart TV do?; **2.** What do you use it for?; **3.** Was it very expensive?

5.3 I know there are no game consoles in the shop.; I've been feeling very weak. I was sick for almost a week.; Is there a phone around here? I can hear it ringing.

5.4 **1.** I / eye; **2.** hi / high; **3.** knew / new; **4.** male / mail

5.5 **1.** I had eight donuts last night.; **2.** I sent my first email this morning.; **3.** He knows how to use a smart TV.; **4.** Don't leave your phone out in the sun.

5.6 The Atlas was built to take part in a competition called the Igor I. Sikorsky Human Powered Helicopter Competition. On 13 June 2013, the team that built it won the competition.

The competition started in 1980 with a prize of $25,000. However, the first teams to take part could only get their helicopter around 20 cm off the ground for a few seconds. People thought the competition was too difficult and for 15 years no one took part in it. The organizers then decided to increase the prize money to $250,000 to attract more competitors. This interested the team from the University of Toronto and they started building the Atlas.

The challenge was to fly a human-powered helicopter three meters off the ground for 60 seconds, while keeping the pilot inside a 10 square-meter area marked on the ground. Each individual part of the challenge had been achieved before, but the Atlas team was the first to do all three at the same time—winning the prize.

6.1 Hello, and welcome to another podcast of *Work-Life Balance*. Today we take a look at stress at the workplace and how we can overcome it.

About 80% of workers feel stress at work, and 19% have quit a job because of stress. The most stressful jobs include pilot and journalist, while the least stressful jobs include professor and librarian.

There are many things that cause work stress. One example is working long hours without a break. Other causes include too much work and worrying about losing your job.

People who are stressed fall sick very often. Some common illnesses that are signs of stress include headaches, tiredness, depression, and weight loss. In more serious cases, stress can result in heart attacks or strokes.

So, how do we reduce stress? First of all, take steps to cut down the number of hours you work. Plan your time well and take short breaks regularly. You could also take up a relaxing hobby or start exercising to decrease stress.

6.2 **1.** On my way to work, I take some deep breaths.; **2.** When a meeting finishes, I listen to relaxing music.; **3.** If I have too much work, I tell my manager.; **4.** I go to the gym after I finish work.

6.3 Carl doesn't worry after exams. / Carl doesn't worry after exams.

6.4 **1.** Did you fail your English exam? / No, I failed my math exam. **2.** Does Andrew study English on Mondays? / No, he studies Spanish on Mondays. **3.** Did you help Sam study for his driving test? / No, I helped Rachel study for her driving test. **4.** Are they going to the movie on Saturday? / No, they are going on Sunday. **5.** Was Simon involved in the accident? / No, his sister was in the accident.

6.5 **1.** Are you meeting David at the coffee shop?; **2.** Does Lee play the guitar?; **3.** Did Julie go to the supermarket?; **4.** Was his mother at the game?

6.6 Hugh Herr has a passion for rock-climbing, and he's been doing it since he was a young boy. By the time he was 17, he was known to be one of the best climbers in the United States.

When Herr was 17, he and a friend were rock-climbing up a mountain when a big snow storm hit. It was hard to see and the boys got lost. They spent three nights in freezing temperatures before they were rescued. When they got to the hospital, doctors discovered they had suffered from terrible frostbite. Both of Herr's legs had to be removed below the knees.

Doctors said he would never be able to climb again. But Herr was determined to prove them wrong. After months of recovery, Herr was climbing again. He designed special legs to help him do this. These legs made him a better climber than he was before the accident because he can change their lengths as he climbs.

Herr also went back to school and became an engineer. He now designs robotic legs for other people with disabilities. He hopes that with technology, people with disabilities will be able to enjoy a new sense of freedom.

7.1 Hi Lisa, it's Angela. You offered to give Sarah a lift to the festival on Saturday. I thought I'd tell you what she looks like—otherwise you might drive off with someone else!

Well, she's short like me—she's about 150 centimeters tall. She has long, brown hair and she wears glasses. She's not too thin, but she's also not too heavy. I think she's quite attractive, and has a beautiful smile. She's one of my best friends, and she's a very friendly person.

She'll be wearing a green coat so you should look out for that too. Hope you guys have fun this Saturday!

7.2

W: Hi, how's it going?

M: Pretty good. Hey, tell me something. Are you in the same class as my friend Steve?

W: Steve? Hmm. I think there are a couple of Steves in my class. What's he like?

M: Well, he's really talkative. He'll talk to anyone about anything. In fact, he never stops talking.

W: Yeah, there is a guy like that. What does he look like?

M: Well, he's got light-colored hair and brown eyes. He's also slim and fairly short.

W: Oh, I know him! He's a really interesting guy.

M: Yeah he is. Maybe the three of us can hang out sometime. It's always fun when Steve's around.

W: Sure! I'd like that.

7.3 She's quite shy.; She is really nice, though.; We're going to the party tomorrow?; Yes, we are going to the party.

7.4 **1.** I know you're not going to the party, but I am.; **2.** It's my first job.; **3.** We are going home now and you're coming too.; **4.** My mother's very strict, but my father is not.; **5.** He's taking a flight tomorrow. He won't miss it.

7.5

A: Oh, hello... Um, I'm the new part-time assistant.

B: Oh great! You must be Paul. Let me show you where you'll be working. Is this your first job?

A: Yes, it is. This is a really exciting day for me.

B: You look a little nervous!

A: Yeah, I am quite nervous!

B: Oh, don't worry. Everything will be fine. Let me know if I can help.

A: Thanks, I will.

7.6 Job interviews can be very stressful experiences. Not only are we worried about getting the job, but we're also afraid of saying or doing the wrong thing. Here are a few tips to help you stay calm and make a good impression.

Before the interview starts, find a private place and do a power pose for two minutes. This will help you feel more confident. When you enter and leave the interview room, make eye contact with the interviewer, smile, and give a firm handshake. However, when shaking hands don't squeeze too hard—it makes some people uncomfortable.

Sit up straight, and look directly at your interviewer, to show you're engaged with them. Leaning forward also makes you appear interested, but don't get too close to other people. Finally, move your hands about occasionally as you talk—it helps you express yourself naturally. Just remember not to wave your hands about wildly.

There are many different things you need to do to pass an interview, and having the right body language is an easy one to get right.

8.1 Last summer, I volunteered to track whales in the Indian Ocean on a boat. My job was to count the number of whales to see how many are left.

Sadly, the number of whales in the Indian Ocean is decreasing. The ocean has lots of beautiful islands, but the water can be kind of dirty. There's a huge pile of garbage that moves around the ocean. That's really sad to see because the whales eat a lot of this garbage thinking it's food. This makes them very sick, and some even die.

The Indian Ocean is still a fascinating place. It's the third-largest ocean in the world, and it stretches between Africa, Asia and Australia. I really want to go back and volunteer again next summer. It was an amazing experience and I also want to find out if whale numbers are increasing.

8.2

M: Hi! How was your vacation?

W: Oh, it was the greatest vacation ever! I spent a whole month traveling around New Zealand.

M: Sounds fantastic! So what did you get up to?

W: Well, I saw lots of natural places. You know, they have some amazing waterfalls out there.

M: Oh, really? Like Niagara Falls?

W: No, not quite that big. The highest falls I saw were Bridal Veil Falls, which were 55 meters high. However, Omaru Falls were more beautiful.

M: That's great! Did you visit any beaches?

W: Yeah, I did. There's a really long one called Ninety Mile Beach, and that was probably the best of all the beaches there. It was so beautiful! There was another good one called Hot Water Beach, but it was much more crowded than the others.

M: Oh no! I can't stand crowded places. So were the beaches the best thing about New Zealand?

W: Oh, everything was so nice, it's hard to pick my favorite. The Sky Tower in Auckland was one of the best places I visited, but I also loved Lake Taupo. I think New Zealand's the most interesting place I've been to.

M: Sounds like you had a great time! You must show me your photos sometime.

8.3 See you tomorrow!; Seeya tomorrow!; Come on, let's go!; C'mon, let's go!

8.4 **1.** going to / gonna; **2.** give me / gimme; **3.** got to / gotta; **4.** get you / getcha; **5.** sort of / sorta; **6.** let me / lemme

8.5 **1.** I'm gonna go to Mexico!; **2.** Lemme guess: You're going with your classmates.; **3.** I wanna explore some caves there.; **4.** It's sorta cloudy today.; **5.** Bye, I've gotta go.; **6.** Can you gimme a lift to the library?

8.6 In March 1974, some farmers were digging a well near Xi'an in China when they made one of the world's greatest discoveries. They had dug to about 15 meters deep, when one of the farmers, Yang Zhifa, found something. It looked like the top of a head, made from clay—a kind of mud. They dug deeper and found a life-sized statue. It looked very old. In fact, the farmers had discovered one of China's greatest historical treasures, the terracotta army.

Archeologists who dug up the site were amazed at the discovery. The army consisted of 8,000 statues of soldiers and horses. Not only were there many soldiers in what seemed to be a huge tomb, they were lined up like real soldiers ready for battle. Each soldier had a unique facial expression—no two were alike. Experts think that the terracotta army was buried with China's first emperor to protect him in the afterlife.

The terracotta army is now a famous attraction. After over 2,200 years of being hidden away, millions of people can see the clay soldiers displayed in major museums around the world.

9.1 Dean Karnazes was born in 1962. He grew up in the small city of San Clemente, California, and started running at a very early age. When he was in kindergarten, he would run back home after school. On his twelfth birthday, he cycled a distance of 64 kilometers just for fun.

Since then, Dean Karnazes has achieved some pretty amazing things in his life. In 2005, he took part in an event and ran for over 80 hours without sleeping. That's three and a half days! In that time, he ran a total distance of 563 kilometers. In 2006, he ran 50 marathons, in 50 states, in 50 days. His achievements earned him the nickname: Ultramarathon Man.

Over the years, Karnazes has inspired thousands of people to become more active—his 50-day marathon was to raise awareness for youth obesity and to motivate people to be more active. *TIME* magazine named him one of the "Top 100 Most Influential People in the World."

9.2 When I was young, I hated running. If you'd told me I was going to run a marathon, I would've laughed at you. But last week, I did it—I ran a marathon in San Francisco! I didn't do it alone though; I ran with my best friend. Quite honestly, I couldn't have done it without her. Why did I do it? Well, it was a marathon to raise money for a charity. We managed to raise $800 for schools in Africa.

We started training six months ago. We ran twice a week, every week. It was really hard at first, but I got used to it. So, how did we do? Well, I finished, but my friend didn't. She hurt her knee and had to stop. I completed the race in about five hours, which is a little slow. I'm delighted that I did it, but I'll never do it again! Maybe next time I'll do something less tiring, like a read-a-thon!

9.3 We started two hours ago because we wanted to end early.

I finished the race in last place and laughed loudly.

As I traveled around the world, I learned many languages.

9.4 **1.** I watched the moon landing on TV.; **2.** The talent show ended two hours ago.; **3.** He sailed around the world alone.; **4.** She walked across Asia and Africa.

9.5 /id/: greeted, lifted, ended; /t/: hoped, washed, liked; /d/: climbed, skied

9.6 Lewis Pugh is a swimmer who cares about the environment. He wants to draw attention to the problems of climate change, pollution, and overfishing. Every time he takes on a new swimming challenge, he tells people about environmental problems in that area and asks people to help save the natural world.

Pugh swam the five oceans to appeal for protected areas in the oceans. When he swam at the North Pole, he wanted to highlight the issue of melting sea ice. Melting ice and rising sea levels pose a very serious problem to the wildlife there. When he swam across Lake Pumori on Mount Everest, he drew attention to the melting of the glaciers in the Himalayas due to climate change.

Pugh often talks to politicians and business leaders about environmental issues. His goal is to get their support to protect the oceans and stop climate change.

10.1 I grew up near a small town called Lincoln. I lived just outside the town, so there was lots of green space, with two parks within ten minutes' walk from my house. The streets were really nice and clean, and the houses were big. Everyone knew each other and my neighbors were really helpful. It was a great place to grow up.

I had to move to the city when I got a job. My new neighborhood is downtown, right in the city center. It's different from my hometown, and some things are definitely worse, like the housing. It's expensive here, whereas back in my old neighborhood it was very affordable. There's also heavy traffic all day and all night. It took me a long time to get used to it, and I couldn't sleep at first.

There are some benefits to living in the city, though. Because I live in an apartment block now, I know all my neighbors and they're really good, friendly people. Another positive thing is that there are lots of restaurants, bars, and cinemas really close. Nights in the city are much more fun than in a small town.

10.2 **1.** Hi, I'm Alice. I love the area where I live except for one thing: it's really far from my job. I live close to my friends and family, the apartment's cheap and the nightlife's wonderful. The thing is it takes me over an hour to get to work, and even longer to get home in the evening. To be honest, I dread going to work because of the journey. What should I do?; **2.** Hey, I'm Carlos. I've lived in the city for about seven years now, but I wonder if it's time for a change. I just feel that living life here is unhealthy. I mean, there's heavy traffic so the air's polluted and there are no parks or green space. It would be great to get some fresh air and see some trees every day. Can you give me some advice, please?; **3.** Hello, I'm Soo-jin. I recently changed my job. I hated my old job, but the money was good. Now I've got my dream job, but it doesn't pay so well. I'm having trouble paying the rent. My apartment's pretty big, and it's downtown, so the rent's quite high. I don't know what to do. Please advise me.

10.3 I live in New York because it's so much fun, and the parks are great.

I wanted to move to Westfield, but the rent was too high.

10.4 Ten years ago, my family moved to this neighborhood because it was cheap. It had a bit of a crime problem and it wasn't very safe. In my opinion, things have improved a lot. It's now a really safe neighborhood with clean streets and excellent schools.

10.5 **1.** The housing isn't very affordable so I'll move to another neighborhood.; **2.** We're trying to improve the neighborhood by cleaning the streets.; **3.** I want to live in the downtown area as the nightlife there is great.; **4.** How about moving to Sydney and getting a new job?

10.6 The city of Providence in Rhode Island, U.S.A., needed some help. One of its downtown neighborhoods was full of ugly, vacant buildings, crime was high and its two rivers were highly polluted. The area's future did not seem bright.

Residents found a surprising answer to the problems. They organized a regular festival in the neighborhood, called WaterFire. WaterFire is an arts festival with live music, fireworks, outdoor theater performances, and displays of paintings. Visitors can eat delicious food while enjoying local culture, or they can take part in the performances themselves. Many boats travel along the rivers during the festival, adding to the excitement.

WaterFire has led to many improvements in the downtown area. After enjoying the festival, people wanted to spend more time in the neighborhood. New shops and businesses started opening, and the neighborhood gained a reputation for being fashionable and fun. Lots of people visited the area for shopping and relaxation. Providence's government responded by building more parks and planting trees. As more people started moving into the area, crime dropped and ugly old buildings were renovated. After some dark years, WaterFire has lit up downtown Providence again.

11.1

W: Wow, there are so many photos in here! Where do we start?

M: I heard this photographer takes hundreds of photos every month. How about we start at this landscape here?

W: Let's read the description… Ah, it's in Germany, and that's a famous castle. It's done from a different perspective though—it looks almost like a painting!

M: I love it! It looks like such a peaceful and romantic place. I can imagine walking through the mountains and swimming in the lake. The colors are gorgeous!

W: I'm not so sure. I think the photographer's made the colors a little too bright. I like the use of light though.

M: Well, let's agree to disagree! Now, how about this next photo?

W: Let's see… It's a portrait of a child holding a soccer ball. He's very dirty, isn't he?

M: He is, isn't he! I think he's been playing soccer in the rain. He looks very happy though. It's a stunning photo, full of life and happiness.

W: Yes, it's a really striking image. I love the way it's only in black and white. It's like the photographer wanted to focus all the attention on the child.

M: I agree! So, shall we move on to the next photo?

▶ 11.2

W: Hey, take a look at this photo on Instagram. It's gorgeous, isn't it? I know it's just a diver with many fish swimming around him, but you can learn so much about nature from it. Look at how the fish move around the diver, like they're one animal. I find it fascinating!

M: Yeah, I suppose so. It's quite good, it's just… Well, I think the colors are all wrong. They look weird. I've been diving before and the ocean doesn't look like that. I wish photographers would keep their images looking natural.

▶ 11.3 That photo's not very pretty. Please take it again. Just take pictures of whatever seems interesting. That's better!

▶ 11.4 thought, bu**tt**er, lot, perspective, le**tt**er, math, exci**t**ing, listen, wri**t**er

▶ 11.5 **1.** I'm eighty years old now.; **2.** I've taken a lot of pictures, thousands.; **3.** My dad let me use his cheap little camera to take a picture of a lake.; **4.** The water looked amazing.; **5.** It was bright and shining like metal.

▶ 11.6 Photography used to be something special, because it was hard to do and it was expensive. Before taking a photo, you had to learn how to use a camera properly, and people took a lot of care over their photos. They framed their shots carefully and waited for the right moment. Now people can just tap a screen and their smartphone does all the work. That's much easier, of course, and it means that anyone can take photos now. However, it also means that the photos are less special, because the artistic skill is gone.

People nowadays take pictures of just about anything—their food, their feet, every place they go, and everything they do. We upload around 2 billion photos to the Internet every day. There are probably a lot of good photos out there, but it's hard to see them because they're lost among the millions of other pictures. We see hundreds of images a day, but how many of those do we actually remember?

▶ 12.1 We all know that exercise is good for us, but most people aren't sure how much exercise they need to do, or how often. Luckily, there are many ways to track your exercise habits and reach your goals.

The first way is by using an exercise app on your smartphone. There are hundreds of exercise apps around nowadays. Running and cycling apps can track your speed and distance, tell you how much energy you've burned, and track your progress. Other apps can replace a fitness trainer, telling you what to do and for how long in order to achieve your goals. Exercise apps are great, however, the downside to using fitness apps is that you have to carry a smartphone with you while you exercise. They're usually quite large and can break easily.

If you don't want to carry a smartphone, you could buy a fitness tracker. It usually looks like a small watch, and it counts how many steps you take and records how quickly your heart beats. It then uses this information to find out how much energy you've burned that day. Fitness trackers are fairly cheap, but they're only useful if you walk or run. If you do other kinds of exercise, the tracker won't recognize it.

If you want the best of both worlds, think about getting a smartwatch. They do everything a fitness tracker does, but they can also use apps, like a smartphone. Unfortunately, they're still pretty expensive and the batteries don't last a long time.

With all of this fitness technology available, it's never been easier to get fit and improve your health.

▶ 12.2

M: Hey, how's the diet going?

W: Well, it was going alright, but I'm finding it hard now. There's just too much delicious food around!

M: Yeah, I know what you mean. I've got a few tips though, if you want to hear them.

W: Sure, go ahead!

M: OK, the first one is: don't eat late at night. You see, you don't use the energy because you're sleeping. Late night snacks are bad!

W: I'd never thought about that. I guess I do eat late. OK, what else?

M: Well, make sure you have breakfast. Then you feel less hungry later in the day.

W: Oh, really? I always skip breakfast. OK, I'll start eating breakfast again.

M: Good! Right, the last tip is to drink water before a meal.

W: Why? What does that do?

M: Well, it makes you feel full. Then you'll want to eat less.

W: Ah, I understand. OK, so don't eat late, remember to eat breakfast and drink plenty of water. Got it!

▶ 12.3

A: Soda contains loads of sugar. You should order something else.

B: Well, how about juice? Or does it contain sugar too?

▶ 12.4 **1.** An exercise buddy can make working out more fun.; **2.** You should always wash your hands before meals.; **3.** You can easily gain weight if you eat late-night snacks.

▶ 12.5 My friend often brushes her teeth just after eating, as she says it makes her mouth feel cleaner. This is actually a mistake. Your mouth is acidic after a meal and brushing then can damage your teeth. Instead, wait 30 minutes after eating before brushing your teeth.

▶ 12.6 We know there are bad habits that damage your teeth, but what are some good habits that will prevent damage? Well, we know that it's best to avoid sugary foods and drinks. However, if you really can't resist sugary drinks, drink them through a straw. That way, the drink won't touch your teeth and won't coat them with sugar. And instead of eating candy, have some fruit for a sweet treat.

If you do eat or drink something sugary, eating cheese afterward is a great way to reduce the acid levels. Chewing sugar-free gum will do the same thing. Wait at least half an hour after eating or drinking, then gently brush your teeth with a soft toothbrush. Using mouthwash is a good idea too, as it will kill bacteria and give you fresh breath.

Finally, try to eat a healthy, varied diet with lots of vitamins and minerals so that your teeth and gums can repair themselves.

Credits

Photo Credits

Cover Diane Cook and Len Jenshel/National Geographic Creative, **3** Pablo Corral Vega/ National Geographic Creative, **9** Robertus Pudyanto/Getty Images Entertainment/Getty Images, **11** (tl) © James Duncan Davidson/TED, (tc) © Photo by Jurvetson on flickr, (tr) © James Duncan Davidson/TED, **18** Tomoji Hirakata/Moment/Getty Images, **23** ZUMA Press, Inc./Alamy, **25** Paul Nicklen/National Geographic Creative, **30** M4OS Photos/Alamy, Lukas Godja/Shutterstock, **32** Alan Welner/AP, **34** (tl) Pascal Deloche/Godong/Corbis Documentary/Getty Images, (tc) Lukas Gojda/Shutterstock, (tr) Computer Arts Magazine/Future/Getty Images, **38** Bill Wymar/ Alamy, **39** SPORTSANDNEWS/SIPA/Newscom, **44** Lucy Pemoni/AP, **46** Rex Features/AP, **51** © James Duncan Davidson/TED, **53** © TED, **56** Richard Nowitz/National Geographic Creative, **58** © Martin Edstrom, **60** © Brent McGregor, **65** © Kelvin Trautman, **67** Handout/Getty Images News/Getty Images, **72** Randy Duchaine/Alamy, **74** Alex Wong/Getty Images News/ Getty Images, **79** evsila/Stockimo/Alamy, **81** Carsten Rehder/dpa/picture-alliance/Newscom, **82** Sean Pavone/Alamy, **86** Galina Barskaya/Shutterstock, **88** © James Duncan Davidson/TED

Text Credits

79 Adapted from "The Visual Village": ngm.nationalgeographic.com, October 2013